Fodor's Pocket Guide to New York City

Theodore Fischer

Fodor's Travel Publications, Inc.
New York and London

ISBN 0-679-01811-5

Fodor's Pocket Guide
to New York City

Editors: Caroline Haberfeld, Holly Hughes
Editorial Contributor: Laura Broadwell
Art Director: Fabrizio La Rocca
Cartographer: David Lindroth
Illustrator: Karl Tanner
Cover Photograph: Owen Franken

Design: Vignelli Associates

Special Sales

Fodor's Travel Publications are available at special discounts for bulk purchases (100 copies or more) for sales promotions or premiums. Special editions, including personalized covers, excerpts of existing guides, and corporate imprints, can be created in large quantities for special needs. For more information write to Special Marketing, Fodor's Travel Publications, 201 East 50th Street, New York, NY 10022. Inquiries from the United Kingdom should be sent to Fodor's Travel Publications, 30–32 Bedford Square, London WC1B 3SG.

MANUFACTURED IN
THE UNITED STATES OF AMERICA
10 9 8 7 6 5 4 3 2 1

Contents

Maps

Foreword

The sheer number of attractions and activities that New York City offers its guests can stagger both the first-time visitor and the experienced traveler. *Fodor's Pocket Guide to New York City* is intended especially for the new or short-term visitor who wants a complete but concise account of the most exciting places to see and the most interesting things to do.

Those who plan to spend more time in New York, or seek additional information about areas of interest, will want to consult *Fodor's New York City* for in-depth coverage of the city.

While every care has been taken to assure the accuracy of the information in this guide, the passage of time will always bring change, and consequently the publisher cannot accept responsibility for errors that may occur.

All prices and opening times quoted here are based on information available to us at press time. Hours and admission fees may change, however, and the prudent traveler will avoid inconvenience by calling ahead.

Fodor's wants to hear about your travel experiences, both pleasant and unpleasant. When a hotel or restaurant fails to live up to its billing, let us know and we will investigate the complaint and revise our entries where the facts warrant it.

Send your letters to the editors of Fodor's Travel Publications, 201 East 50th Street, New York, NY 10022.

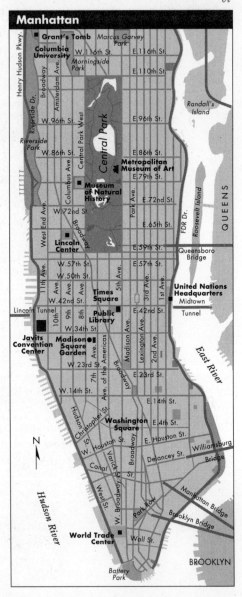

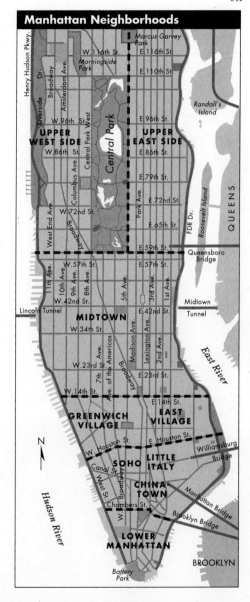

viii

Introduction

Whatever you're looking for in a big-city vacation, you'll find in New York.

The city has history: You can trace the life of the early Dutch settlers, canny traders who, unconstrained by religious strictures of fellow colonists in Massachusetts and Pennsylvania, gave the city its enterprising soul. You can see the spot where George Washington was sworn in as first U.S. president, the grave of Alexander Hamilton, and the restored site of America's greatest 19th-century seaport.

The city has architecture: "New York" and "skyline" are virtually a single word. But along with a succession of buildings that, in their time, ranked as the world's tallest structures (the Flatiron, Woolworth, Chrysler, and Empire State buildings, and the World Trade Center Towers), New York retains many handsome residential reminders of its Colonial and Victorian past. Contemporary architectural treasures range from the bizarre (Guggenheim Museum) to the sublime (Trump Tower) to the perplexingly postmodern (AT&T Building).

No one has to make a case for New York's performing arts. In show-biz terms, the Big Apple is top banana. A New York street by the name of Broadway is an international adjective for theater. The Metropolitan Opera, New York Philharmonic, and New York City Ballet are national companies. Their greatness is nurtured by the talent of hundreds of non-Broadway theaters, musical ensembles, and dance troupes—all performing nightly in New York. The city remains the world center of jazz, rock, and dance music attuned to every generation.

New York has a full complement of professional sports organizations: two baseball teams (Mets and Yankees), two football teams (Giants and Jets), two basketball teams (Knicks and New Jersey Nets), and three hockey teams (Rangers, Islanders, New Jersey Devils). It's easy to find a boxing or wrestling match. And horse races, both thoroughbred and standardbred, are off and running almost every day of the year at one of the four area tracks.

Perhaps because New York lacks the outdoor endowments of other locales, the city places a stronger emphasis on the joys of the table. New York has 17,000 restaurants, some world famous institutions, others the "in" spots of the day, neighborhood standbys, or back-street discoveries.

Even though the island of Manhattan has largely become a river-to-river high-rent district, its ethnic neighborhoods thrive. Little Italy, Chinatown, and other pockets of ethnicity are not theme parks but vibrant, ever-changing areas that remain magnets for Old Country settlers.

S ome New York attractions occupy a class by themselves. The Statue of Liberty, the Brooklyn Bridge, the Empire State Building, Times Square, and Central Park may be situated in New York City, but all belong to the world.

Above and beyond the laundry list of sights and activities, New York has an undefinable aura that exists nowhere else. It's a kind of energy level that has something to do with being in the big league, where everybody's watching and keeping score.

Part of the big-league mentality derives from the kind of industries headquartered here. New York has Wall Street, the financial center of the world. It contains the corporate headquarters of major TV networks, most national magazines, book publishers, and news-gathering organizations. The largest advertising agencies and public relations firms are here. New York also has the fashion industry and the United Nations. A lot goes on here, and a lot of people are around to tell about it.

Walking down a New York street, you might pass Henry Kissinger (with a bodyguard or two). You could go into a restaurant and get a table across from Robert DeNiro. You are very likely to turn to a corner and see a feature film or TV series being filmed. And even if you don't see someone you recognize, you always feel that you just *might*. Paraphrasing a slogan coined for The Plaza hotel, you get the feeling that "nothing unimportant ever happens in New York," and it lends an edge to everything that goes on.

You may already have heard that New York can be an expensive place in which to live or to visit. New York hotels are among the country's most costly, and the price ranges of Manhattan restaurants seem to be a couple of levels above those one finds elsewhere in the country. Movie tickets, museum admissions, clothing, drinks, incidentals—many things cost more here. Yet there are shopping bargains in New York; those things that New York produces, such as books, can often be found at much lower prices here than in the other 49 states.

And there is crime, which can occur in the most unexpected places. The person who appears to have an accident at the exit door of a bus is in reality a pickpocket who will flee with your wallet or purse if you attempt to give aid. The individual who approaches you with a complicated story about having "found" money or other valuables is playing a confidence game and hopes to get something from you. Violent crime can occur anywhere, at any hour, and the only reasonable precautions anyone can take are to keep jewelry and valuables out of sight on the street and to walk generally on the main thoroughfares, with the crowds. Women should never hang a purse on a chair in a restaurant or on a hook in a restroom stall.

New Yorkers themselves often appear to be brusque, haughty, cold, even rude in their manner. This is largely a defensive attitude that residents develop, consciously or not, to cope with living so closely with so many other people. When you encounter rudeness, don't take it personally; it's just that individual's way of behaving. And when you have the opportunity to talk for a bit with New Yorkers, you'll find that they usually warm to you and will often go out of their way to be accommodating.

Many are the tales of visitors lost on the subway who are shepherded to safety by a Good Samaritan from Canarsie. Strangers constantly come forward to mediate disputes between out-of-towners and cab drivers. Ask New Yorkers for simple directions and they're likely to tell you a lot more than you need to know. New Yorkers can be as down-to-earth as people anywhere. Yet they can also be brash, opinionated, impatient, smug, self-important, and, in a peculiar way, maddeningly provincial. As O. Henry wrote, "What else can you expect from a town that's shut off from the world by the ocean on one side and New Jersey on the other?"

America's greatest metropolis presents the visitor with a superfluity of opportunity. You can't do it all; you don't have the time, and nobody has the money. So you will have to make decisions, and the big one will probably be whether you see what New York does best or you do the things that you like best. On the whole, that's a great choice to have.

1 Essential Information

Before You Go

Visitor Information

In North America. Contact **The New York Convention and Visitors Bureau** (2 Columbus Circle, New York, NY 10019, tel. 212/397–8222) and the **New York Division of Tourism** (1 Commerce Plaza, Albany, NY 12245, tel. 800/225–5697 or 518/474–4116). Ask for the *I Love New York* series of booklets.

Tips for British Travelers

Passports and Visas You will need a valid passport (cost £15). You do not need a Visa if you are staying for fewer than 90 days, have a return ticket, and are flying with a major airline. There are some exceptions to this, so check with your travel agent or with the United States Embassy (Visa and Immigration Dept., 5 Upper Grosvenor St., London W1A 2JB, tel. 01/499–3443). No vaccinations are required.

Customs Visitors 21 or over can take in 200 cigarettes or 50 cigars or 3 pounds of tobacco; 1 U.S. quart of alcohol; duty-free gifts to a value of $100. Be careful not to take in meat or meat products, seeds, plants, fruits, etc. Avoid illegal drugs like the plague.

Returning to Britain you may bring home: (1) 200 cigarettes or 100 cigarillos or 50 cigars or 250 grams of tobacco; (2) two liters of table wine with additional allowances for (a) one liter of alcohol over 22% by volume (38.8° proof, most spirits), (b) two liters of alcohol under 22% by volume, or (c) two more liters of table wine; and (3) 50 grams of perfume and 1/4 liter of toilet water, and (4) other goods up to a value of £32.

Insurance We recommend that you insure yourself to cover health and motoring mishaps. **Europ Assistance** (252 High St., Croydon, Surrey CR0 1NF, tel. 01/680–1234).

It is also wise to take out insurance to cover loss of luggage (though check that this isn't already covered in an existing homeowner's policy). Trip-cancellation insurance is another wise buy.

The Association of British Insurers (Aldermary House, Queen St., London EC4N 1TT, tel. 01/248–4477) will give comprehensive advice on all aspects of vacation insurance.

Tour Operators Most tour operators now offer excellent budget packages to the U.S. Among those to consider are

Albany (Manchester) Ltd. (190 Deansgate, Manchester M3 3WD, tel. 061/833–0202).

American Airplan (Marlborough House, Churchfield Rd., Walton-on-Thames, Surrey KT12 2TJ, tel. 0932/246166).

Thomas Cook Ltd. (Box 36, Thorpe Wood, Peterborough PE3 6SB, tel. 0733/503202).

Jetsave (Sussex House, London Rd., East Grinstead RH19 1LD, tel. 0342/312022).

Pan Am/Fly Drive (193 Piccadilly, London W1V 0AD, tel. 01/409–3377).

Speedbird (152 King St., London W6 0QU, tel. 01/741–8041).

Airfares We suggest that you explore the current scene for budget flight possibilities. Unfortunately, there are few standby programs on any of the major airlines, but do check their APEX and other fares, which offer a considerable saving over the full price. Quite frankly, only some business travelers who don't have to watch the price of their tickets fly full-price these days— and find themselves sitting right beside an APEX passenger! At press time, an APEX round-trip fare to New York cost from £299. The small daily and Sunday newspaper ads are also a good source of bargain price flights. As we went to press, round-trip bargain flights cost around £199.

Information One excellent source of information is the **State of New York Division of Tourism** (25 Bedford Sq., London WC1B 3HG, tel. 01/323–0648). Although they are not open for personal callers, they will be happy to send brochures and other information.

What to Pack

Pack light because porters and luggage trolleys are hard to find. Luggage allowances on domestic flights vary slightly from airline to airline. Most allow three checked pieces and one carry-on. Some give you the option of two checked pieces and two carry-ons. In general, check-in luggage may not weigh more than 70 pounds each or be larger than 62 inches (length + width + height). Carry-on luggage may not be larger than 45 inches (length + width + height) and must fit under the seat or in the overhead luggage compartment.

New York City has many restaurants that require a jacket and tie. For sightseeing and casual dining, jeans and sneakers are acceptable just about anywhere in the city. Sneakers seem to be the universal walking shoe, especially among women, regardless of whether they are wearing business suits, shorts, or slacks. New York can be very cold in the winter, but there's not much snow. The humidity level tends to be high in summer, so leave the plastic raincoats at home.

Cash Machines

Virtually all U.S. banks belong to a network of ATMs (Automatic Teller Machines), which dispense cash 24 hours a day in cities throughout the country. There are some eight major networks in the United States, the largest of which are Cirrus, owned by MasterCard, and Plus, affiliated with Visa. Some banks belong to more than one network. These cards are not automatically issued; you have to ask for them. Cards issued by Visa and MasterCard may also be used in the ATMs, but the fees are usually higher than the fees on bank cards, and there is a daily interest charge on the "loan," even if monthly bills are paid on time. Each network has a toll-free number you can call to locate machines in a given city. The Cirrus number is 800/4–CIR-RUS; the Plus number is 800/THE–PLUS. Check with your bank for fees and for the amount of cash you can withdraw on any given day.

Car Rentals

We cannot urge you strongly enough to avoid bringing a car into Manhattan. Street parking is extremely scarce (violators are towed away literally within minutes), garages cost as much as $15 for two hours in some neighborhoods, and daytime Manhattan gridlock can fray the calmest nerves.

That said, you may still need a car, perhaps for a weekend escape or because Manhattan is part of a longer trip. New York offers an unusually confusing array of car rental possibilities. The old ploy of renting out of Newark Airport to take advantage of lower rates no longer works. Prices charged by major national firms are the same at Newark, Kennedy, and LaGuardia airports, as well as at Manhattan rental locations. Expect to pay $45–$55 per day with 70–100 free miles and 30¢ per additional mile for a subcompact. Companies with multiple Manhattan and airport locations include: **Dollar** (tel. 800/421-6868), **Budget** (tel. 800/527-0700), **Thrifty** (tel. 800/367-2277), **National** (tel. 800/328-4567), **Hertz** (tel. 800/654-3131), and **Avis** (tel. 800/331-1212). Some regional budget companies like **American International** (tel. 800/527-0202) offer lower rates; so does **Rent-A-Wreck** (tel. 800/221-8282). If you are flying into LaGuardia or Kennedy, you might look into some local Queens agencies with lower rates, such as **ABC** (tel. 800/247-6110) or **Universal** (tel. 718/786-0786). **Sunshine Rent-A-Car** (tel. 212/989-7260) is good for budget rentals in Greenwich Village.

Whomever you rent from, get a reservation number and ask if there is free mileage and if you must pay for a full tank of gas whether you use it or not. Also, find out what you're responsible for if you don't sign a collision-damage waiver; this can add $9–$12 daily to your bill. Be aware that many rental companies are redefining customer responsibility to include loss of the car from theft or vandalism.

Arriving and Departing

By Plane

The Airlines Virtually every major U.S. and foreign airline serves one or more of New York's three airports: *LaGuardia Airport, John F. Kennedy International Airport,* and *Newark International Airport.*

When choosing a flight, be sure to distinguish among (a) *nonstop flights*—no stops or changes of aircraft; (b) *direct flights*—one or more stops but no change of aircraft; (c) *connecting flights* —at least one change of aircraft and possibly several stops as well.

Airlines serving the New York area include: America West (tel. 800/247–5692), American (tel. 800/433–7300), Braniff (tel. 800/272–6433), Continental (tel. 800/525–0280), Delta (tel. 800/ 221–1212), Midway (tel. 800/621–5700), Northwest (tel. 800/225–2525), Pan Am (tel. 800/442– 5896), Piedmont (tel. 800/251–5720), TWA (tel. 800/221–2000), United (tel. 800/241–6522), and USAir (tel. 800/428–4322).

Smoking Federal regulations currently forbid smoking on all flights scheduled to last two hours or less —about 80% of all flights within the United States. On longer flights, U.S. airlines must provide a seat in the nonsmoking section to any passenger who requests one. Passengers, however, must comply with airline check-in requirements, which means checking in 10–20 minutes before scheduled departure time. In addition, Northwest Airlines has banned smoking on its domestic flights. There are several bills pending in Congress that would extend the two-hour ban to all domestic flights.

From Airports to Center City **LaGuardia Airport** is in the borough of Queens, eight miles northeast of midtown Manhattan. Taxis cost $12–$18 plus toll (up to $2) and take 20–40 minutes. Group taxi rides to Manhattan are available at taxi dispatch lines just outside the baggage claim areas during most travel hours (no service Saturdays or holidays). Group fares range from $7–$9 per person (plus share of tolls), depending on your destination. Call 718/784-4343 for more information.

Carey Airport Express (tel. 718/632-0500) buses depart for Manhattan every 20–30 minutes from 6:45 AM to midnight. It's a 20–30 minute ride to 42nd Street and Park Avenue, directly opposite Grand Central Terminal. A shuttle bus runs from here to the New York Hilton, Sheraton City Squire, and Marriott Marquis hotels. To other midtown hotels, it's a short cab ride. The bus fare is $7.50; pay the driver. **Giraldo Limousine** serves major Manhattan hotels direct to and from the airport. The fare is $9 per person; make arrangements at the ground transportation center or use the courtesy phone.

John F. Kennedy International Airport (JFK) is in the borough of Queens, 15 miles southeast of midtown. Taxis cost $24–$30 plus tolls (up to $2) and take 35–60 minutes.

Carey Airport Express (tel. 718/632-0500) buses depart for Manhattan from all JFK terminals every 20–30 minutes, 6 AM to midnight. The ride takes about one hour to 42nd Street and Park Avenue (Grand Central Terminal). A shuttle bus runs from here to the New York Hilton, Sheraton City Squire, and Marriott Marquis hotels; it's a short cab ride to other midtown hotels. The bus fare is $8; pay the driver. **Giraldo Limousine** serves major Manhattan hotels directly from the airport; the cost is $12 per person. Make arrangements at the ground transportation counter or use the courtesy phone.

The **JFK Express** is a special subway service from the Howard Beach station near JFK Airport to downtown Brooklyn, lower Manhattan, Greenwich Village, and Midtown, terminating at 57th Street and Sixth Avenue. Shuttle buses from JFK terminals to the Howard Beach station depart every 20 minutes from 6:03 AM to 12:52 AM. The ride to the 57th Street terminus takes 50 minutes. Trains have luggage space and plenty of transit police. The fare is $6.50, including connection to the entire subway system; pay on the train. (To reach JFK, you pay $1 to enter the subway system and an additional $5.50 on board the train.)

Newark International Airport is in Newark, New Jersey, 16 miles southwest of Midtown. Taxis cost $28–$30 plus tolls ($3) and take 20–45 minutes. "Share and Save" group rates are available for up to four passengers between 8 AM and midnight; make arrangements with the taxi dispatcher.

NJ Transit Airport Express buses depart every 15–30 minutes for the Port Authority Terminal, at 42nd Street and Eighth Avenue. From there it's a short cab ride to midtown hotels. The ride takes 30–45 minutes. The fare is $7; buy your ticket inside the terminal. The **Olympia Trails Express Bus** to the World Trade Center and Grand Central Terminal departs every 20 minutes from 5 AM to midnight.

The travel time to the World Trade Center is 20 minutes; to Grand Central, 35 minutes. The fare is $6; pay the driver. **Newark Airport/NYC Minibus** departs for major Manhattan hotels about every 30 minutes, but schedules vary according to passenger demand. The fare is $12; make arrangements at the ground transportation counter.

By Car

The **Lincoln Tunnel** (I–495), **Holland Tunnel**, and **George Washington Bridge** (I–95) connect to the New Jersey Turnpike system and points west. The Lincoln Tunnel leads to midtown Manhattan, the Holland Tunnel to lower Manhattan, the George Washington Bridge to northern Manhattan. Each of the three arteries requires a toll ($3 for cars) eastbound into New York, but no toll westbound.

From Long Island, the **Midtown Tunnel** (I–495) and **Triborough Bridge** (I–278) are the most direct arteries to Manhattan. Both require tolls ($2 for cars) in both directions.

From upstate New York, the city is accessible via the **New York (Dewey) Thruway** (I–87) (toll) and the **Major Deegan Expressway** (I–87) through the Bronx and across the **Triborough Bridge** (toll).

From New England, the **Connecticut Turnpike** (I–95) connects to the **New England Thruway** (I–

95) (toll), the **Bruckner Expressway** (I–278), and the **Triborough Bridge** (toll) to upper Manhattan.

Be forewarned: Driving within Manhattan can be a nightmare of gridlocked streets and predatory fellow motorists. Free parking is almost impossible to find in Midtown and parking lots are exorbitant—$16 for three hours is not unusual in midtown lots—all over town. If you do drive, don't plan to use your car much for driving within Manhattan.

By Train

Amtrak (tel. 800/872–7245) offers frequent service within the Northeast Corridor, between Boston and Washington. Trains arrive and depart from Pennsylvania Station (31st to 33rd Sts., between Seventh and Eighth Aves.). Amtrak trains also serve Penn Station from the Southeast, Midwest, and Far West.

Amtrak service from Montreal and upstate New York and the Lake Shore Limited from Chicago both use Grand Central Terminal (42nd St. and Park Ave.).

Metro-North Commuter Railroad (tel. 212/532–4900) serves Grand Central from the northern suburbs and Connecticut as far east as New Haven. The **Long Island Railroad** (tel. 718/454–5477) has service from all over Long Island to Penn Station. Also at Penn Station, **New Jersey Transit** (tel. 201/460–8444) offers frequent service from the north and central regions of the state.

By Bus

All long-haul and commuter bus lines feed into the **Port Authority Terminal,** a mammoth multi-level structure that occupies a nearly two-square-block area between 40th and 42nd streets and Eighth and Ninth avenues. Though it's recently modernized and fairly clean, the large number of vagrants make the terminal an uncomfortable place to spend much time. Especially on night arrivals, plan to move swiftly through the terminal.

For information on any service into or out of the
Port Authority Terminal, call 212/564–8484.
Some of the individual bus lines serving New
York include **Greyhound-Trailways** (consult local
information for a number in your area), **Adirondack** and **Pine Hill Trailways** from upstate
New York (tel. 914/339–4230); **Bonanza Bus
Lines** from New England (tel. 401/331–7500);
Martz Trailways from northeastern Pennsylvania (tel. 717/829–6911); **Peter Pan Bus Lines**
from New England (tel. 413/781–2900); and **Vermont Transit** from New England (tel. 802/862–
9671).

Staying in New York City

Important Addresses and Numbers

Tourist Information The **New York Convention and Visitors Bureau**
at Columbus Circle (58th St. and Eighth Ave.)
provides a wealth of free information, including
brochures, subway and bus maps, listings of hotels and weekend hotel packages, and discount
coupons for Broadway shows. Drop in or, better
yet, contact them before you arrive. *2 Columbus
Circle, New York, NY 10019, tel. 212/397–8222.
Open weekdays 9–6, weekends 10–6. Closed holidays.*

Emergencies 911 for **police, fire,** or **ambulance** in an emergency.

Doctor **Doctors On Call, 24-hour housecall service** at
212/737–2333. Near Midtown, 24-hour emergency rooms are open at **St. Luke's–Roosevelt
Hospital** (458 W. 59th St., tel. 212/523–4000)
and **St. Vincent's Hospital** (Seventh Ave. and
11th St., tel. 212/790–7000).

Dentist The **Dental Emergency Service** (212/679–3966;
after 8 PM, tel. 212/679–4172) will make a referral.

24-Hour Pharmacy **Kaufman's Pharmacy** (Lexington Ave. and 50th
St., tel. 212/755–2266).

Getting Around

New York is a city of neighborhoods best explored at a leisurely pace, up close, and by foot. But New York neighborhoods are big, and you'll need some motorized means of travel between them.

By Subway The 300-mile subway system is the fastest and cheapest way to get around the city. It operates 24 hours a day and, especially within Manhattan, serves most of the places you'll want to visit. The New York subway also deserves many of the negative aspects of its image. Even though new graffiti-proof, air-conditioned cars predominate now, many trains are crowded, dirty, noisy, somewhat unreliable, and occasionally unsafe. Unsavory characters lurk in the stations, and panhandlers, who are noisy but usually harmless, work their way through the cars. Don't write off the subway—it really is colorful, and millions ride it every day without incident—but stay alert at all times.

The subway costs $1, with reduced fares for the disabled and seniors at all hours. You must use a token to enter. They are sold at token booths that are *usually* open at each station. It's advisable to stock up on tokens since the token booth may not be open and, if open, may have a long line. You can also use tokens on city buses. A token permits unlimited transfers within the subway system.

Free subway maps are given out at token booths upon request. They are often out of stock, so ask at several booths until you find one. Maps are also posted in subway cars but are seldom found on platforms. Make sure you refer to an up-to-date map; lengthy repair programs often cause reroutings that last long enough for new "temporary" maps to be printed.

For route information, ask the token clerk or a transit policeman. And don't hesitate to ask directions from any knowledgeable-looking fellow rider: Once New Yorkers realize you're harmless, they bend over backward to help. For 24-hour information, call 718/330–1234. (Calls from the 212 area code to 718, and vice versa, cost the local rate, 25¢ from pay phones.)

A few words on safety: Most of the stops in Midtown are crowded with riders all hours of the day or night. Stay among those crowds—there's safety in numbers. Don't wander off to a deserted section of the platform and don't enter empty or nearly empty cars. At off-peak hours, try to ride in the same car as the conductor; it will stop near a line of light bulbs above the edge of the platform. Follow the crowd until you reach the comparative safety of the street.

By Bus Most buses follow easy-to-understand routes along the Manhattan grid. Routes go up or down the north-south avenues, east and west on the major two-way crosstown streets. Most bus routes operate 24 hours, but service is infrequent late at night. Buses are great for sightseeing, but traffic jams—a potential threat at any time or place in Manhattan—can make rides maddeningly slow.

Bus fare is $1 in change only (no pennies) or a subway token. When you get on the bus you can get a free transfer good for one change to an intersecting route. Legal transfer points are listed on the back of the transfer. Transfers have time limits of at least two hours, often longer. You cannot use the transfer to enter the subway system.

Each of the five boroughs of New York has a separate bus map, and they are scarcer than hen's teeth. They are occasionally available in subway token booths and never available on buses. Your best bets are the Convention and Visitors Bureau at Columbus Circle or the information kiosks in Grand Central Terminal and Penn Station.

By Taxi Taxis are usually easy to hail on the street or from a line in front of major hotels. Taxis cost $1.15 for the first 1/8 mile, 15¢ for each 1/8 mile thereafter, and 15¢ for each minute not in motion. A 50¢ surcharge is added to rides begun between 8 PM and 6 AM. There is no charge for extra passengers. Taxi drivers also expect a 15% tip. Barring performance above and beyond the call of duty, don't feel obliged to give them more.

To avoid unhappy taxi experiences, be sure to have a general idea of where you want to go. Some cab drivers are dishonest; some are ignorant; some can barely understand English. In any case, if you don't have any idea of the proper route, you may be taken for a long and costly ride.

New York taxis are mile-for-mile less expensive than in many places, and in some instances taxis can be a bargain. A short trip for two or more people may cost less than the combined bus or subway fare.

Jogging The principal area for jogging is Central Park, a runner's paradise from dawn till sundown. A 1.59 mile soft surface track rings the Reservoir (Fifth Ave. and 90th St.). For information on group runs, call the **Road Runners Club** (tel. 212/860–4455).

Bicycling You can rent bikes in Central Park from **Central Park Bicycle Rental,** located beside the Loeb Boathouse parallel to 72nd Street (tel. 212/861–4137). Outside but near the park, you can rent bikes from **Metro Bicycles** (1311 Lexington Ave. at 88th St., tel. 212/427–4450); **Midtown Bicycles** (360 W. 47th St., tel. 212/581–4500); and **West Side Bicycle** (231 W. 96th St., tel. 212/663–7531).

Guided Tours

Orientation Tours The most pleasant way to get a crash orientation to Manhattan is aboard a **Circle Line Cruise.** Once you've finished the three-hour 35-mile circumnavigation of Manhattan, you'll have a good idea of where things are and what you want to see next. Narrations are as interesting and individualized as the guides—often moonlighting actors—who deliver them. *Pier 83, west end of 42nd St., tel. 212/563–3200. Fare: $15 adults, $7.50 children under 12. Operates daily, early Mar. through Nov.*

At South Street Seaport's Pier 16 you can take two- or three-hour voyages to New York's past aboard the iron cargo schooner, *Pioneer* (tel. 212/669–9416). You can take 90-minute tours of New York Harbor aboard the sidewheeler *Andrew Fletcher* or the re-created steamboat *DeWitt Clinton* (tel. 212/669–9400).

For a shorter excursion, the **TNT Express,** a new hydroliner, will show you the island of Manhattan in only an hour. *Pier 11, south of South Street Seaport, tel. 212/244–4770. Fare: $18 adults, $16 senior citizens, $10 children under 12, under 5 free. Boats depart weekdays 11 AM and 2 PM, weekends 10, 12, and 2 PM.*

The Gray Line (900 Eighth Ave. at 53rd St., tel. 212/397–2600) offers a number of different city bus tours, plus cruises and day trips to Brooklyn, and Atlantic City. **Short Line Tours** (166 W. 46th St., tel. 212/354–5122) offers a number of tour options. **Manhattan Sightseeing Bus Tours** (150 W. 49th St., tel. 212/869–5005) has 10 different tours.

Island Helicopter (Heliport at E. 34th St. and East River, tel. 212/683–4575) offers a number of flyover options, from $30 (for 16 miles) to $139 (for over 100 miles). From the west side, **Manhattan Helicopter Tours** (heliport at W. 30th St. and Hudson River, tel. 212/247–8687) has tours from $35 to $144.

Special-Interest Tours

Backstage on Broadway (tel. 212/575–8065) takes you behind the scenes of a Broadway show and lets you mingle with show people. Reservations are mandatory. **Art Tours of Manhattan** (tel. 609/921–2647) provides an inside view of museum and gallery exhibits. **Gallery Passports** (tel. 212/288–3578) admits you to artists' studios and lofts and other art attractions near Manhattan. **Soho Art Experience** (tel. 212/219–0810) offers tours of Soho's architecture, galleries, shops, and artists' lofts. **Doorway to Design** (tel. 212/221–1111) tours fashion and interior design showrooms, as well as artists' private studios. **Harlem Your Way!** (tel. 212/690–1687) offers daily walking tours and Sunday gospel trips to one of the most exciting areas of the city.

Walking Tours

Sidewalks of New York (33 Alan Terr., Suite #2, Jersey City, NJ 07306, tel. 212/517–0201) hits the streets from various thematic angles—Historic Church Tours, Ye Old Tavern Tours, Celebrity Home Tours, Final Resting Places of the Rich and Famous Tours. Tours are offered on weekends, both days and evenings, year-round. Tours last 2–2½ hours and cost $10; no reservations are required. **Adventure on a Shoestring**

(300 W. 53rd St., New York, NY 10019, tel. 212/
265–2663) is a 27-year-old organization that ex-
plores unique New York neighborhoods. Tours
are scheduled periodically, $5 per person. **The
Municipal Art Society** (tel. 212/935–3960) operates a series of bus and walking tours. The
Urban Park Rangers (tel. 212/397–3080) offers
weekend walks and workshops, most of them
free, in city parks. The **92nd Street YMHA** (tel.
212/996–1105) always has something special to
offer on weekends.

The most comprehensive listing of tours offered
during a particular week is published in the
"Other Events" section of *New York* magazine.

Self-Guided The **New York Convention and Visitors Bureau**
Walking Tours provides three pamphlets that cover historical
and cultural points of interest in Manhattan and
Brooklyn: the "I Love New York Visitors Guide
and Map," "42nd Street–River to River," and
"Brooklyn on Tour." The materials are available
at the bureau's information center (2 Columbus
Circle, tel. 212/397–8222).

The **Municipal Art Society of New York** has prepared a comprehensive "Juror's Guide to Lower
Manhattan: Five Walking Tours" for the benefit
of jurors who are often required to kill a lot of
time while serving in downtown courthouses.
Along with an explanation of the New York jury
system, the pamphlet includes tours of Lower
Manhattan and Wall Street; City Hall District;
Chinatown and Little Italy; South Street Seaport; and TriBeCa. Jurors get copies free;
nonjurors can purchase copies at Urban Center
Books (457 Madison at 51st St., New York, NY
10022, tel. 212/935–3595).

A free "Walking Tour of Rockefeller Center"
pamphlet is available from the information desk
in the lobby of the RCA Building (30 Rockefeller
Plaza).

2 Exploring New York City

Orientation

Visitors finding their way their way around
the city soon discover that Manhattan has a Je-
kyll-and-Hyde personality. Rational Dr. Je-
kyll dwells above 14th Street, where the streets
form a regular grid pattern. Avenues run north
(uptown) and south (downtown). Streets run
east and west (crosstown). The exceptions are
Broadway, a diagonal from 14th to 79th streets,
and the thoroughfares along the Hudson and
East rivers.

Fifth Avenue (originally Middle Road) is the
baseline: Street addresses begin at Fifth Avenue and increase in regular increments. East of
Fifth, the addresses 1–99 E. are between Fifth
and Park avenues; 100–199 E. between Park and
Third avenues; 200–299 E. between Third and
Second avenues; and so on. West of Fifth Avenue, the addresses 1–99 W. are between Fifth
and Sixth avenues; 100–199 W. between Sixth
and Seventh avenues; 200–299 W. between Seventh and Eighth avenues; and so on. Above 59th
Street, West Side addresses begin at Central
Park West, an extension of Eighth Avenue.

Avenue addresses are much less regular. The
building numbers begin wherever the avenue
begins, and they increase by irregular increments. An address at 552 Third Avenue, for
example, will not be at the same cross street as
(or necessarily anywhere near) 552 Second Avenue or 552 Lexington Avenue. Avenue addresses given in this book (and in many other listings)
include both the number and the nearest cross
street, for example, "303 Lexington Avenue at
37th Street." When you don't know the nearest
cross street, you can calculate the location of an
avenue address by referring to the formulas in
the Manhattan Address Locator.

Below 14th Street, Manhattan streets reflect
the disordered personality of Mr. Hyde. They
are either diagonals aligned with present or
long-gone shorelines or the twisting descen-
dants of an ancient cow path. Below 14th Street
you will encounter such anomalous situations as
the intersection of West 4th Street and West
11th Street, the misunderstandings caused by

Manhattan Address Locator

To locate avenue addresses, take the address, cancel the last figure, divide by 2, add or subtract the key number below. The answer is the nearest numbered cross street, approximately. To find addresses on numbered cross streets, remember that numbers increase east or west from 5th Ave., which runs north–south.

Ave. A... *add 3*

Ave. B...*add 3*

Ave. C...*add 3*

Ave. D...*add 3*

1st Ave....*add 3*

2nd Ave....*add 3*

3rd Ave....*add 10*

4th Ave.... *add 8*

5th Ave.

Up to 200...*add 13*

Up to 400...*add 16*

Up to 600...*add 18*

Up to 775...*add 20*

From 775 to 1286...

cancel last figure and

subt. 18

Ave. of the

Americas...*subt. 12*

7th Ave....*add 12*

Above 110th St... *add 20*

8th Ave....*add 9*

9th Ave....*add 13*

10th Ave....*add 14*

Amsterdam

Ave....*add 59*

Audubon Ave....*add 165*

Broadway

(23–192 Sts.)...*subt. 30*

Columbus Ave....*add 60*

Convent Ave....*add 127*

Central Park West...

divide house number by

10 and add 60

Edgecombe

Ave....*add 134*

Ft. Washington

Ave....*add 158*

Lenox Ave....*add 110*

Lexington

Ave....*add 22*

Madison Ave....*add 27*

Manhattan

Ave....*add 100*

Park Ave....*add 34*

Park Ave.

South...*add 8*

Pleasant

Ave....*add 101*

Riverside Drive...

divide house number

by 10 and add 72 up to

165 Street

St. Nicholas

Ave....*add 110*

Wadsworth

Ave....*add 173*

West End Ave....*add 59*

York Ave....*add 4*

the proximate and roughly parallel Greenwich Street and Greenwich Avenue, the transformation of Leroy Street into St. Luke's Place for one block before reverting to Leroy, and the general confusion engendered by East Broadway, West Broadway, and just plain Broadway.

Logic won't help you below 14th Street; only a good street map and good directions will.

You may also be confused by the way New Yorkers use "uptown" and "downtown." These terms refer both to locations and to directions. Uptown means north of wherever you are at the moment; downtown means south. Yet uptown and downtown are also geographical areas of the city. Unfortunately, there is no consensus about where these areas are: "Downtown" may mean anyplace from the tip of Lower Manhattan through Chelsea; it depends on the orientation of the speaker.

A similar situation exists with "East Side" and "West Side." Someone may characterize a location as being "on the East Side," meaning somewhere east of Fifth Avenue. A hotel described as being "on the West Side" may be located on West 42nd Street. But when many New Yorkers speak of the East Side or the West Side, they have in mind the respective areas above 59th Street (the southern boundary of Central Park), on either side of the park. Admittedly, the usage is not precise; you should be prepared for misunderstandings.

Tour 1. Midtown: Rockefeller Center

Numbers in the margin correspond with points of interest on the Midtown Manhattan map.

❶ The heart of midtown Manhattan is **Rockefeller Center,** a complex of 19 buildings occupying nearly 22 acres of prime real estate between Fifth and Seventh avenues and 47th and 52nd streets. Built during the Great Depression of the 1930s by John D. Rockefeller, Jr., this city-within-a-city is the capital of the communications industry, with the headquarters for a TV network (NBC), major publishing companies (Time-Life, McGraw-Hill, Simon & Schuster, Warner Brothers), and the world's largest news-gathering organization, the Associated Press. It is an international center housing the consulates of many foreign nations, the U.S. passport office, and ticket offices for numerous airlines. Most human needs—restaurants, shoe repair, doctors, barbers, banks, post office, bookstores, clothing, variety stores—can be accommodated within the center, and all parts of the complex are linked by underground passageways.

Begin a tour at the ice rink on **Lower Plaza** along a little street called Rockefeller Plaza between 49th and 50th streets. Crowned by a gold-leaf statue of Prometheus stealing the sacred fire for mankind, this famous New York attraction is an ice rink from late September through April and an outdoor cafe the rest of the year. The site of a huge Christmas tree and caroling concerts during December, Lower Plaza is surrounded by the flags of all the members of the United Nations. Incidentally, those "Private Street, No Parking" signs along Rockefeller Plaza aren't jokes: This really is a private street that must be closed to both cars and pedestrians one day a year to maintain its private status.

Just east of Lower Plaza are the **Channel Gardens,** a promenade with six pools surrounded by flower beds filled with seasonal plantings, conceived by artists, floral designers, and sculptors —10 shows a season. They are called Channel Gardens because they separate the British building (to the north) and the French building (to the south). The French building contains the **Librairie de France,** which sells French-language books, periodicals, and records; its surprisingly large basement contains a Spanish bookstore and dictionary store.

A huge statue of Atlas supporting the world stands sentry before the **International Building** on Fifth Avenue between 50th and 51st streets. With a lobby inspired by ancient Greece and fitted with Grecian marble from the island of Tenos, the building houses foreign consulates, international airlines, and a passport office from which lines of applicants overflow into Fifth Avenue throughout the summer.

❷ Across Fifth Avenue stands the Gothic-style **St. Patrick's,** the Roman Catholic cathedral of New

York. Dedicated to the patron saint of the Irish —then and now one of New York's principal ethnic groups—the white marble and stone structure was begun in 1858, consecrated in 1879, and completed in 1906. Among the statues in the alcoves around the nave is a striking modern rendering of the American saint, Mother Seton.

One of Rockefeller Center's main attractions is the **RCA Building,** the 70-story tower that occupies the block bounded by Rockefeller Plaza, Avenue of the Americas (which New Yorkers call Sixth Avenue), and 49th and 50th streets. The building is headquarters for NBC. One way to see what goes on up there is to request free tickets to the NBC shows that are produced in New York—currently *Late Night with David Letterman, Saturday Night Live,* and *Donahue* —by writing NBC Tickets, 30 Rockefeller Plaza, New York, NY 10112. (Unfortunately, the first two shows are booked solid for more than a year in advance, *Donahue* for about six months.) Or you might take a tour of the NBC studios: One leaves every 15 minutes, 9:30–4:30, Monday through Saturday, and Sundays during the summer (cost: $7). And you can buy a T-shirt, ashtray, frisbee, or other paraphernalia bearing logos from your favorite programs at a boutique in the magnificent black granite lobby. Look up at the ceiling mural above the Rockefeller Plaza entrance: The figure seems to be facing you no matter where you stand.

Those who are intent on seeing network TV should look around Rockefeller Center for pages distributing tickets to screenings of TV shows contemplated for broadcast by NBC (tel. 212/664–7174), CBS (tel. 212/975–2476), and ABC (212/887–3537). On some weekdays, pages stand on the sidewalks buttonholing passersby for screenings that normally begin within an hour or two.

Escalators in the RCA Building will take you to the marbled catacombs that connect the various components of Rockefeller Center. A lot goes on down under: There are restaurants in all price ranges, from the chic American Festival Café, alongside the skating rink, to McDonald's; the

Midtown Manhattan

W. 58th St.
W. 57th St.
W. 56th St.
W. 55th St.
W. 54th St.
W. 53rd St.
W. 52nd St.
W. 51st St.
W. 50th St.
W. 49th St.
W. 48th St.
W. 47th St.
W. 46th St.
W. 45th St.
W. 44th St.
W. 43rd St.
W. 42nd St.
W. 41st St.
W. 40th St.
W. 39th St.
W. 38th St.
W. 37th St.
W. 36th St.
W. 35th St.
W. 34th St.
W. 33rd St.
W. 32nd St.
W. 31st St.
W. 30th St.
W. 29th St.
W. 28th St.
W. 27th St.
W. 26th St.
W. 25th St.
W. 24th St.
W. 23rd St.
W. 22nd St.
W. 21st St.
W. 20th St.
W. 19th St.
W. 18th St.
W. 17th St.
W. 16th St.
W. 15th St.

Tenth Ave.

Ninth Ave.

Eighth Ave.

Eleventh Ave.

Twelfth Ave.

Dyer Ave.

THEATER DISTRICT

Port Authority Bus Terminal

Javits Convention Center

Lincoln Tunnel

Post Office

CHELSEA

Hudson River

N

Rockefeller Center Museum; a post office and clean public washrooms (both scarce in Midtown); and just about every kind of store. To find your way around, consult the strategically placed directories or obtain the free "Shops and Services Guide" at the RCA Building reception desk. *Center*, a free quarterly magazine containing articles about Rockefeller Center, a calendar of events, and capsule descriptions of the restaurants, is available in the lobbies of most of the buildings.

Across 50th Street from the RCA Building is America's largest indoor theater, the 6,000-seat **Radio City Music Hall.** Home of the fabulous Rockettes chorus line (which actually started out in St. Louis in 1925), Radio City was built as a movie theater with live shows; today it produces concerts, Christmas and Easter extravaganzas, awards presentations, and other special events. When there's no show you can tour the premises for $6 (tel. 212/632–4041).

Components of the Rockefeller Center community along Sixth Avenue include the 51-story **McGraw-Hill Building** (Sixth Ave. between 48th and 49th Sts.). Its lower plaza contains a 50-foot steel sun triangle that points to the seasonal positions of the sun at noon, and a pool that demonstrates the relative size of the planets.

Time Out For supercasual eating when the weather is good, the **Sixth Avenue food vendors** near Rockefeller Center offer the best selection in the city. Most à la "cart" diners eschew the hot dog as being too pedestrian when they can just as easily have tacos, falafel, souvlaki, tempura, Indian curry, Afghani kofta kebabs, or Caribbean beef jerky. Locations change periodically, so look around until you find what you like. Food carts are licensed and inspected by the Department of Health. And the price is right; no dish is more than $5, and most cost much less. For seating, perch on the benches and low walls in the plazas beside the massive Sixth Avenue office towers.

Heading east again, 53rd Street between Sixth and Fifth avenues is a mini Museum Row. The ❸ **American Craft Museum** spotlights the work of contemporary American and overseas craftspersons working in clay, glass, fiber, wood, metal, paper. *40 W. 53rd St., tel. 212/956-3535. Admission: $3.50 adults, $1.50 students and seniors; free Tues. 5-8. Open Tues. 10-8; Wed.- Sun. 10-5.*

❹ The **Museum of Modern Art** (MOMA) is a bright and airy four-story structure built around a secluded sculpture garden. All the important movements of modern art are represented here. After only a quick look-see, you'll be able to drop terms like Cubism, Surrealism, Abstract Expressionism, Minimalism, and Postmodernism as though you've known them all your life. Some of the world's most famous paintings are hung on the second floor: Van Gogh's *Starry Night*, Picasso's *Les Demoiselles d'Avignon*, Matisse's *Dance*. The superstars of American art appear on the third floor: Andrew Wyeth, Andy Warhol, Jackson Pollock, Frank Stella, Mark Rothko—to name a few. Don't miss the classic office furniture and Paris subway bench in the fourth-floor Architecture and Design Collection. Afternoon and evening film showings, mostly foreign films and classics, are free with the price of admission; tickets are distributed in the lobby, and on some days they go fast. Programs change daily; call 212/708-9490 for a schedule. *11 W. 53rd St., tel. 212/708-9500. Admission: $6 adults, $3.50 students, $3 seniors, free under 16. Pay what you wish Thurs. 5-9. Open daily 11-6; Thurs. 11-9; closed Wed.*

❺ The **Museum of Broadcasting** presents periodic screenings, usually retrospectives of the work of a particular radio or TV star or of an era in broadcasting history. The museum also offers its stupendous collection of more than 30,000 TV and radio programs for individual screening. *1 E. 53rd St., tel. 212/752-7684. Suggested contribution: $4 adults, $3 students, $2 seniors and under 13. Open Tues. noon-8; Wed.- Sat. noon-5.*

Tour 2. Midtown: Fifth Avenue

The stretch of Fifth Avenue between Rockefeller Center and 57th Street glitters with world-famous shops. The list begins with **Saks Fifth Avenue** (Fifth Ave. and 50th St.), the flagship of the national chain. Another big-name store is **Gucci**—actually two Guccis, on adjacent corners of Fifth Avenue and 54th Street. **Bijan** (699 Fifth Ave.) sells wildly expensive men's Continental clothing—by appointment only. Health warnings and no-smoking ordinances notwithstanding, **Nat Sherman** (711 Fifth Ave.) continues to market his own brands of cigarettes, cigars, and smoking accessories from his clubby shop.

Steuben Glass occupies a ground-floor showroom of a green-glass tower at Fifth Avenue and 56th Street. Across the street, **Harry Winston** (718 Fifth Ave.) has fabulous jewelry but does not encourage browsers. **Tiffany & Co.** (727 Fifth Ave., at 57th St.) is less intimidating and perhaps somewhat less expensive than you may fear.

Take a serenity break in **St. Thomas's Church** (Fifth Ave. at 53rd St.), an Episcopal institution that has occupied the site since 1911. The impressive huge stone reredos behind the altar holds the statues of more than 50 apostles, saints, martyrs, missionaries, and church figures. Upon entering, look to the far right to see enameled discs representing the branches of the armed forces and carved busts of four U.S. military chiefs-of-staff.

❻ A block east, on Madison Avenue and 55th Street, you can pop into the post-deregulation home of Ma Bell in the new **AT&T World Headquarters.** Unlike the sterile ice-cube-tray buildings of Sixth Avenue, AT&T's rose granite columns, its regilded statue of the winged *Golden Boy* in the lobby, and its peculiar Chippendale roof have earned it its sobriquet as the first postmodern skyscraper. An adjacent structure houses the **AT&T InfoQuest Center,** a postmodern museum of communications technology. Entrants receive an access card on which they encode their names and then use to operate displays on lightwave communication, microelectronics, and computer software. Displays are neither terribly technical nor (on behalf of AT&T) zealously self-serving. Some exhibits, such as those where you program your own music video and rearrange a scrambled pic-

ture of your face, are downright entertaining.
*Madison Ave. and 56th St., tel. 212/605–5555.
Admission free. Open Wed.–Sun. 10–6; Tues.
10–9.*

Cross 56th Street to the **IBM Building,** with its
fragrant and inviting public atrium *(see* Public
Spaces). A passage connects it to its next-door
neighbor, but you'll do better to walk around the

❼ corner and encounter **Trump Tower** through the
grand Fifth Avenue entrance. Trump Tower is
an exclusive 68-story, dark glass apartment
house. What's open to the public is a six-story
shopping atrium paneled in pinkish-orange marble and trimmed with high-gloss brass. A
fountain cascades against one wall, drowning
out the clamor of the city. In further contrast to
the real world, every inch of Trump Tower is
kept gleamingly shined, and security is omni-
present but discreet. Shops are chic and tony,
among them Cartier, Bucellati, and Abercrom-
bie & Fitch, and the public restrooms in the
basement are invitingly clean and spacious.

Time Out **Terrace V,** so named because it occupies a corner
of the fifth level of Trump Tower, is a delightful
place for simple entrees, elaborate sandwiches,
imaginative salads, and a glass of good wine. On
nice days you can sit outdoors on a bright terrace overlooking the street; indoor seating rates
a pleasant view of the atrium. The prices aren't
cheap, but neither are the surroundings.

Tour 3. Midtown: 57th Street

Don't consider hunting for bargains in the exclusive shops and galleries of 57th Street. A recent
survey determined that merchants here paid the
world's highest ground-floor retail rents: $425
per square foot, edging out Tokyo's Ginza ($400)
and Fifth Avenue between 52nd and 58th
streets ($375). In general, the high costs are
passed along to the consumer.

Occupying the span of Fifth Avenue between
57th Street and the Plaza Hotel, **Bergdorf Goodman** contains designer boutiques and a surprisingly complete men's department. **Van Cleef
& Arpels** jewelers is located within Bergdorf's

57th Street corner. **Bonwit Teller** takes up the
57th Street side of Trump Tower.

Buy the classic trenchcoat with the distinctive
plaid lining straight from the source, at no savings whatsoever, at **Burberry's Ltd.** (9 E. 57th
St.). **Hermès** (11 E. 57th St.) is a small, dignified, and intermittently chic Paris leather shop.
The **Wally Findlay Gallery** (17 E. 57th St.) specializes in 20th-century works, and the **Pace**
Gallery (32 E. 57th St.) features brand-name
(Picasso, Calder, Julian Schnabel) modern and
contemporary artists.

Across Madison Avenue, the **André Emmerich**
Gallery (41 E. 57th St.), in the Art Deco Fuller
Building (note the bronze doors, the marble fix-
tures, the mosaic walls), displays major works
by major modern artists. The least expensive
French designer footwear at **Maud Frizon** (49 E.
57th St.) begins at $100. **Louis Vuitton** (51 E.
57th St.) stamps its familiar "LV" monogram on
its luggage, which it produced first for the
ocean-liner crowd and later for the jet set. Best
known now for the catalogue through which it
distributes gizmos for people who can afford
anything, **Hammacher Schlemmer** (147 E. 57th
St.), founded in 1848, has stood at this spot since
1926.

In two sleekly Art Deco subterranean levels,
❽ the recently opened **Place des Antiquaires** (125
E. 57th St.) is an ultra-high-class shopping mall
where several dozen of the city's top art and antiques dealers operate out of plate-glass stalls.
Some shops have specialties: **Lune** sells almost
nothing but antique fans. You may find the
prices out of your league but, as anywhere, it
costs nothing to look.

When you've had your fill of shopping, walk to
❾ 58th Street and head east across **Sutton Place**
until you can go no further. There you will find
the romantic spot overlooking the East River
and the Queensboro (or 59th Street) Bridge
where Woody Allen and Diane Keaton talked
the night away in *Manhattan.* Cinema trivia
buffs please note that no bench presently occupies the precise spot where Woody and Diane
sat; however, several benches in Sutton Place

Park, a small terrace several steps below, afford
a comparable view.

Tour 4. Midtown: 42nd Street

⑩ Crossroads of the World, Great White Way, the
New Year's Eve Capital of America, **Times
Square** remains one of New York's principal
energy centers. Like most New York City
"squares," Times Square is a triangle, this one
formed by Broadway, Seventh Avenue, and
42nd Street. The square itself is occupied by the
former Times Tower, now simply **One Times
Square Plaza.** On its roof, workmen still lower
the 200-pound New Year's Eve ball down the
flagpole by hand, just as they have since 1908.

⑪ At Duffy Square, on 47th Street between
Broadway and Seventh Avenue, the **TKTS
booth** of the Theater Development Fund sells
half-price (plus $1.50 per ticket service charge)
day-of-performance tickets to Broadway and
Off-Broadway shows. Signboards on the front of
the booth list the shows available that day, and
the offerings fluctuate greatly. Some nights (or
matinees) it seems that almost every show in
town is up for grabs; at other times there may be
nothing but a few long-running hits and some
sleepers. The lines may look long, but they move
surprisingly fast. TKTS accepts only cash or
traveler's checks. *Tel. 212/354–5800. Open 10–2
for Wed. and Sat. matinees; 3–8 for evening performances; noon–8 for Sun. matinee and
evening shows. TKTS booths are open earlier in
the day at 2 World Trade Center and in front of
Borough Hall in Brooklyn.*

Most Broadway theaters are located on the
streets west of Broadway from 52nd Street to
44th Street. The offices of **The New York Times**
(229 W. 43rd St.), the institution that gave the
area its name, occupy much of the block between
Seventh and Eighth avenues.

42nd Street is the title of a long-running musical
(and an earlier movie) that evokes the glamour
and excitement of the New York stage. Today a
group of thriving Off-Broadway playhouses
west of Ninth Avenue are the only live theater
on 42nd Street; the block between Seventh and

Eighth avenues that was once the heart of the
theater district is now a disreputable strip of
porno shops, movie houses, and loiterers, all
marking time while the city assembles the
pieces of a redevelopment project that will
transform the area. The most prominent ves-
tige of the now legendary 42nd Street is the
New Amsterdam (214 W. 42nd St.), a designated
landmark that opened in 1903. Today the New
Amsterdam is "dark," but in its prime the opulent facility, with a second, rooftop theater,
showcased the likes of Eddie Cantor, Will Rogers, Fanny Brice, and the Ziegfeld Girls.

Heading east on 42nd Street, you'll pass
Hotaling's News (142 W. 42nd St., tel. 212/840–
1868), where the front compartment of the bustling little shop carries more than 220 daily
newspapers from throughout the USA, the publications generally only a day or two old. The
rear section stocks current newspapers, magazines, and foreign language books from more
than 40 countries.

Bryant Park and the New York Public Library
occupy the entire block bounded by 42nd Street,
Fifth Avenue, 40th Street, and Sixth Avenue.
Named for the poet and editor William Cullen
Bryant (1794–1878), Bryant Park was the site of
America's first World's Fair, the Crystal Palace
Exhibition of 1853–1854. In recent years, new
landscaping and tightened security have re-
claimed what had come to be a hangout for
undesirables. The long-term future of the park
is still in question.

12 Inside the park, along 42nd Street, **Bryant Park
Half-Price Tickets** sells same-day tickets for music and dance performances throughout the city.
Like theater TKTS, they go for half-price, plus
$1.50 per ticket service charge, cash or travel-
er's checks only. *Open Tues., Thurs., Fri.
noon–2 and 3–7; Wed. and Sat. 11–2 and 3–7;
Sun. noon–6; tel. 212/382–2323 for daily listings.*

Time Out   A cafeteria on the 18th floor of the **City University Graduate Center** provides a serene setting for
a reasonably priced repast, from a snack or

salad-bar salad to a full meal. *33 W. 42nd St., tel. 212/642-2013. Open weekdays 10-8.*

A ground-level passage through the building, connecting 42nd and 43rd streets, often contains art exhibits: Walk through it and behold the offices of *The New Yorker* magazine at 25 W. 43rd Street.

⑬ The central research building of the **New York Public Library** is one of the largest research libraries in the world. Ascend the sweeping staircase between the two crouching Tennessee marble lions—dubbed "Patience" and "Fortitude" by former Mayor Fiorello LaGuardia, who visited the facility to "read between the lions"—and you enter a distinguished achievement of Beaux Arts design (note the triple bronze front doors), an art gallery, and a museum. The research hub of the 85-branch New York Public Library system, the main building displays a Gilbert Stuart portrait of George Washington, Charles Dickens's desk, and Jefferson's own handwritten copy of the Declaration of Independence. Periodic exhibitions focus on literary matters. Free one-hour tours, each as different as the library volunteer who leads it, are given Monday through Saturday at 11 AM and 2 PM. *Tel. 212/930-0800. Open Mon.-Wed. 10-9, Thurs.-Sat. 10-6.*

⑭ Continue east on 42nd Street to **Grand Central Terminal** (never "station," since all runs begin or end here). Constructed between 1903 and 1913, this Manhattan landmark was originally designed by a Minnesota architectural firm and later gussied up with Beaux Arts ornamentation. Make sure you notice the three huge windows separated by columns, and the Beaux Arts clock and sculpture on the facade above 42nd Street. The 12-story ceiling of the cavernous Main Concourse displays the constellations of the Zodiac. You're not likely to overlook the world's largest photographic slide, on the east wall of the concourse, which is changed periodically by Kodak.

Two facilities of note stand at adjacent corners of Park Avenue and 42nd Street, directly opposite Grand Central. On the southwest corner, the **Whitney Museum of American Art at Philip Morris** (120 Park Ave.) occupies the ground floor of the Philip Morris Building. Each year this free branch of the Whitney *(see* Upper East Side) presents five successive exhibitions of 20th-century painting and sculpture. An espresso bar and seating areas make it a much more agreeable place to rest and reconnoiter than anywhere in Grand Central.

The second floor of the building on the southeast corner of 42nd Street and Park Avenue houses ticket counters for most major U.S. airlines. Buses to three New York airports depart from just outside the Park Avenue entrance. Around the corner is the main office of the **Bowery Bank** (110 E. 42nd St.), whose massive arches and 70-foot-high marble columns give it the grand presence of a medieval castle.

Ask New Yorkers to name their favorite skyscraper, and the response you'll hear most often will be the **Chrysler Building** at 42nd Street and Lexington Avenue. The Chrysler Corporation itself is long gone, yet the graceful shaft that culminates in a stainless steel point still captivates the eye and the imagination. The building has no observation deck, but you can examine the elegant dark lobby faced with African marble and covered with a ceiling mural that honors transportation and human endeavor.

Time Out   The **Automat** at the southeast corner of Third Avenue and 42nd Street is the last survivor of the world's first fast-food chain. Patrons use coins or tokens to extract dishes—baked beans and macaroni and cheese are perennial favorites —from glass-fronted cubbyholes, and they crank their coffee out of fish-head spouts. Authentic automat facilities are confined to one wall (a cafeteria, sandwich bar, and bakery occupy most of the space), but the sleek contours of Art Deco styling prevail throughout.

New York's biggest-selling newspaper is produced in the **Daily News Building** (220 E. 42nd St.), an Art Deco tower designed with brown-brick spandrels and windows to make it seem loftier than its 37 stories. The lobby features a revolving illuminated globe, 12 feet in diameter.

The floor is a gigantic compass on which bronze lines indicate air mileage from principal world cities to New York. A small gallery displays *News* photos.

❼ The **Ford Foundation Building** (320 E. 43rd St.) encloses a 12-story, one-third acre greenhouse. With a terraced garden, a still pool, and a couple dozen full-grown trees as centerpieces, the Ford garden is open to the public—for tranquility, not for picnics—weekdays from 9 to 5.

Climb the steps along 42nd Street between First and Second avenues to enter **Tudor City,** a self-contained complex of a dozen buildings in the Tudor Gothic style, featuring half-timbering and lots of stained glass. Constructed between 1925 and 1928, the apartments of this residential enclave originally had no east-side windows, lest the tenants be forced to gaze at the slaughterhouses, breweries, and glue factories then located along the East River.

Walk north across the overpass above 42nd Street and turn east on 43rd Street until the street ends in a terrace overlooking the United Nations Headquarters. The terrace stands at the head of the Sharansky Steps (for Natan, formerly Anatoly, the Soviet dissident), which run along the Isaiah Wall (inscribed, "They Shall Beat Their Swords Into Plowshares"), and overlooks Ralph J. Bunche Park (for the black American former UN undersecretary) and Raoul Wallenberg Walk (for the Swedish diplomat and World War II hero).

❽ The **United Nations Headquarters** complex occupies a lushly landscaped riverside tract along First Avenue between 42nd and 48th streets. A line of flagpoles with banners representing the current roster of 159 member nations stands before the striking 550-foot slab of the Secretariat Building. The interior corridors overflow with imaginatively diverse artwork donated by member nations. Free tickets to most sessions are available on a first-come, first-served basis 15 minutes before sessions begin; pick them up in the General Assembly lobby. Visitors can take early luncheon in the Delegates Dining Room or eat anytime in a public coffee shop. *Tel. 212/963–7539. One-hour tours leave the General Assem-*

bly lobby every 20 minutes, daily 9:15–4:45.
Admission: $4.50 adults, $2.50 students, chil-
dren under 5 not permitted.

Tour 5. Midtown: South of 42nd Street

The gateway to the city for Amtrak passengers
and commuters from New Jersey and Long Is-
(19) land, **Penn Station** is a convenient place to begin
a tour of lower Midtown. However, it is not in itself a particularly felicitous spot. Unattractive,
unsavory, and underground, it serves as an em-
barrassing reminder of the grand old Penn
Station that fell to the wrecking ball in 1963. (If
you arrive in New York at Penn Station, do not
under any circumstances surrender your bag-
gage to the characters hovering about its many
exits: They are not porters; their business is ex-
tortion and theft.)

Madison Square Garden (tel. 212/563–8300),
here in its fourth incarnation, is located directly
above Penn Station. Home of the New York
Knickerbockers (pro basketball) and the New
York Rangers (pro hockey), the Garden lights up
almost every night with dog and cat shows, college basketball, wrestling, rock concerts, cir-
cuses, and other events and expositions; boxing
takes place in the smaller Felt Forum. One of the
last remaining bowling alleys in Manhattan, the
48-lane Madison Square Garden Bowling Center, is located just above the ticket office.

Head north from Penn Station on Seventh Avenue, and you enter New York's tumultuous
Garment District: Street signs declare the
stretch of Seventh Avenue between 31st and
41st streets "Fashion Avenue." The Garment
District teems with warehouses, workshops,
and showrooms that manufacture and finish
mostly women's and children's clothing. On
weekdays the streets are crowded with trucks
and the sidewalks swarm with daredevil
deliverymen hauling garment racks between
factories and subcontractors.

(20) Perhaps to inspire the garment dealers, **Macy's,**
the world's largest department store under one
roof, occupies the entire block bounded by
Broadway, Seventh Avenue, and 34th and 35th
streets. Made world-famous by *Miracle on 34th*

Street and as the destination of the Thanksgiving Day parade, Macy's is still good for a few surprises: At the gourmet food shop in The Cellar, someone is usually distributing free samples of something good to eat (lower level). Other popular spots are the New York, New York souvenir boutique (first floor); the Metropolitan Museum gift shop (mezzanine); and Center Stage Recording Studio, where you can record yourself singing over the instrumental tracks of your favorite hits (fourth floor).

With the demise of the New York Gimbels, the only other major retail enterprise on Herald Square is **Herald Center** (Sixth Ave. and 34th St.), a vertical shopping mall reputedly owned by the footloose Imelda Marcos. Each level of the streamlined center bears the name of a New York neighborhood (SoHo, Greenwich Village, etc.); most stores are high-toned branches of national chains (Ann Taylor, Ylang Ylang, Caswell-Massey).

㉑ Continue east on 34th Street to **B. Altman & Company** (Fifth Ave. and 34th St.). With solid wood counters, high ceilings, and stately white columns, Altman still looks the way all downtown department stores once looked. Compared to the frenetic excesses of Bloomingdale's and Macy's, the spacious and subdued Altman store may strike you as being underpopulated and understocked.

Time Out Altman's eighth-floor **Charleston Garden Restaurant** re-creates the genteel spirit of the Old South, with wrought-iron furniture and the pillared facade of an antebellum mansion. Popular with Altman's older female regulars, Charleston Garden is a calming venue for moderately priced soups, salads, sandwiches, and quiche.

㉒ The **Empire State Building** may no longer be the world's tallest, but it is certainly the world's best-loved skyscraper. The Art Deco playground for King Kong opened in 1931 after only a year and a half of construction. More than 15,000 people work in the building, and more than 1.5 million people a year visit the 86th-floor and 102nd-floor observatories. At night the top 30 stories are illuminated with colors appropriate to the season (red and green around Christmas; orange and brown for Halloween); the lights are doused at midnight to protect bird migration. *Fifth Ave. and 34th St., tel. 212/736–3100. Admission: $3.50 adults, $1.75 children under 12. Open daily 9:30–midnight.*

㉓ Continue south on Fifth Avenue to 29th Street and the **Marble Collegiate Church** (1854), a marble-fronted structure built for the Reformed Protestant Dutch Congregation first organized in 1628 by Peter Minuit, the canny Dutchman who bought Manhattan from the Indians for $24. In modern times the church was the pulpit for Dr. Norman Vincent Peale *(The Power of Positive Thinking)*, its pastor from 1932 to 1984.

㉔ Go east on 29th Street to the **Church of the Transfiguration** (1 E. 29th St.), which is much better known as the Little Church Around the Corner. Set back in a shrub-filled New York version of an old English churchyard, it won its memorable appellation in 1870 when other area churches refused to bury an actor and colleague of the well-known thespian Joseph Jefferson. Jefferson was directed to the "little church around the corner" that did that sort of thing, and the Episcopal institution has welcomed literary and show-biz types ever since.

㉕ Bordered by Fifth Avenue, Broadway, Madison Avenue, 23rd and 26th streets, **Madison Square** was the site (circa 1845) of New York's first baseball games. Though recently rehabilitated with modern sculpture, new benches, and a playground, the most interesting aspects of Madison Square are found along its perimeter.

The block at 26th Street and Madison Avenue, now occupied by the ornate **New York Life Insurance Building,** was the site of the second (1890–1925) Madison Square Garden. The old Garden was designed by the architect and playboy Stanford White, who was shot on the Garden roof by Harry K. Thaw, the jealous husband of the actress Evelyn Nesbit. This lurid episode was more or less accurately depicted in the movie *Ragtime*, scenes of which were filmed on the then-cobblestoned street in front of the **Appellate Division of the State Supreme Court** (Madison Ave. and 25th St.). The roof balustrade of this imposing, white-marble Corinthian structure depicts great lawmakers of the past: Moses, Justinian, Confucius, and others. **The Metropolitan Life Insurance Tower** (Madison Ave. between 23rd and 24th Sts.) re-creates the campanile of St. Mark's in Venice.

The Renaissance-style **Flatiron Building** occupies the triangular lot formed by Broadway, Fifth Avenue, and 23rd Street. Soon after the three-sided 20-story skyscraper was built in 1902, it became a symbol of New York on the rise. Now it lends its name to the Flatiron District that lies to the south, an area of photographers' studios, residential lofts, and advertising agencies.

Continue down Broadway and turn east on 20th Street to the **Theodore Roosevelt Birthplace,** a reconstructed Victorian brownstone where Teddy lived until he was 15 years old. Before becoming President, Roosevelt was New York City police commissioner and the governor of New York State. The house contains Victorian period rooms and Roosevelt memorabilia; a selection of videos about the namesake of the teddy bear are shown on request. *28 E. 20th St., tel. 212/260–1616. Admission: $1. Open Wed.–Sun. 9–5.*

Next door to Roosevelt's home is an interesting shop called **Darts Unlimited, Limited** (30 E. 20th St.), which sells nothing but professional English darts, dartboards, patches, and other dart accessories.

Time Out **Miss Kim's** typifies a kind of dining establishment unique to Manhattan. At this combination grocery store, salad bar, and cafeteria, you obtain your food from a huge 50-item salad table ($3.49 per pound), sandwich bar, steam table with hot foods, pastry counter, or directly from the shelves. Countermen serve hot drinks (including espresso); you take cold drinks (including beer) straight from the cooler. After you weigh and pay, you can either take your meal out or climb to seats on a mezzanine. Similar places exist all over town. *270 Park Ave. S. Open 24 hrs.*

Just east of Park Avenue South, between 20th
(27) and 21st streets, lies **Gramercy Park,** a picture-
perfect city park complete with flower beds,
bird feeders, sundials, cozy benches, and a statue of the actor Edwin Booth portraying Hamlet.
It stays nice because it's surrounded by a locked
cast-iron fence and only residents of the property around the park possess keys. Laid out in
1831 according to a design inspired by London's
residential squares, Gramercy Park is surrounded by interesting structures.

Begin at the northeast corner and head clock-
wise. The white terra-cotta apartment building
at 36 Gramercy Park East is guarded by concrete knights in tarnished armor. The turreted
red-brick building at 34 Gramercy Park East
was one of the city's first apartment houses. The
austere gray Friends Meeting House at 28 Gramercy Park South has lately become The
Brotherhood Synagogue.

Mrs. Stuyvesant Fish, a society doyenne remembered as the fearless iconoclast who
reduced the time of formal dinner parties from
several hours to 50 minutes, resided at No. 19.
Edwin Booth lived at No. 16, now an affiliation
of show-biz people called The Players Club. The
site of the **National Arts Club** (15 Gramercy Park
South) was the home of Samuel Tilden, a governor of New York and the Democratic
presidential candidate who in 1876 received
more votes than Rutherford B. Hayes, who won
the presidency.

Return to Park Avenue South and continue south
(28) to **Union Square,** the area between Park
and Broadway, 14th and 17th streets. During
the early part of the century, Union Square was
a popular patch of green and the site of political
demonstrations. Over the years it deteriorated
into a habitat of drug dealers and kindred undesirables, until a massive renewal program in the
1980s transformed it into one of the city's most
attractive miniparks.

If possible, visit Union Square on greenmarket days (Wednesday, Friday, Saturday), when
farmers from all over the Northeast bring their
goods to the big town. Farmers, including some
Pennsylvania Dutch and latter-day hippies, sell

their own produce, homemade baked goods, cheeses, cider, New York State wines, even fish and meat. If the prices aren't much lower than those in stores, the quality and freshness are much greater. When the weather allows, the benches of Union Square make a great site for a city-style picnic.

Tour 6. Upper West Side

Numbers in the margin correspond with points of interest on the Upper West Side map.

Diversity may be the quality that best characterizes the Upper West Side. A once-fashionable district that had become a multiethnic neighborhood of families and intellectuals, the Upper West Side now attracts young professionals who can afford to live anywhere. Lincoln Center is the cultural anchor, Columbus Avenue the newly fashionable boutique and restaurant strip. Many of the old residents decry the changes that have befallen the neighborhood, but then contentiousness is another characteristic of the Upper West Side.

❶ The West Side story begins at **Columbus Circle,** where a statue of Christopher himself crowns a stately pillar at the intersection of Broadway, Eighth Avenue, Central Park West, and Central Park South. Columbus Circle is a good place to begin any tour of New York, for it is the location of the **New York Convention and Visitors Bureau.** Count on the bureau for brochures; bus and subway maps; hotel, restaurant, and shopping guides; a seasonal calendar of events; free TV-show tickets and discounts for Broadway shows; and sound advice. The New York City Department of Cultural Affairs operates an art gallery on the second floor. *2 Columbus Circle, tel. 212/397–8222. Open weekdays 9–6.*

Central Park West Walk north from Columbus Circle along Central Park West and you quickly reach the haunted apartment house of the film *Ghostbusters* (55 Central Park West at 66th St.). Just inside the park, at 67th Street, is **Tavern on the Green,** a landmark spot for romantic indoor and outdoor dining. The stretch of Central Park roadway between the restaurant and the verdant Sheep

Meadow is the finish line for the New York Marathon (the first Sunday in November). It's also the start and finish of a five-mile "fun run" that begins on the stroke of the New Year.

❷ The stately **Dakota** presides at the corner of Central Park West and 72nd Street. One of the first fashionable West Side apartment buildings, this powerful, relatively squat structure is now better known as the place where *Rosemary's Baby* was filmed and John Lennon was shot. Directly across Central Park West, a hilly stretch of parkland has been designated **Strawberry Fields** in Lennon's memory. A black-and-white-tile mosaic containing the word "Imagine," another Lennon song title, is embedded in one of the paths.

❸ The city's oldest museum, the **New-York Historical Society,** preserves what was unique about the city's past, including the quaint hyphen in New-York. Along with changing exhibits of American history and art, the museum displays original Audubon watercolors, early American toys, Tiffany lamps, antique vehicles, and Hudson River School landscapes. There is an important research library on the second floor. *170 Central Park West, tel. 212/873-3400. Admission: $2 adults, $1.50 seniors, $1 children; pay what you wish Tues. Open Tues.–Sun. 10–5.*

❹ The **American Museum of Natural History,** the adjacent **Hayden Planetarium,** and the surrounding grounds take up a four-block tract bounded by Central Park West, Columbus Avenue, and 77th and 81st streets. With a collection of more than 36 million items, the museum certainly has something for every taste, from a 94-foot blue whale to the 563-carat Star of India sapphire. The Naturemax Theater projects films on a giant screen. The Hayden Planetarium (on 81st Street) has two stories of exhibits, and the Sky Shows are projected on 22 wraparound screens. The rock Laser Shows draw crowds of teenagers Friday and Saturday nights. *Tel. 212/769-5100. Suggested contribution: $3.50 adults, $1.50 children; free Fri. and Sat. after 5. Open daily 10–5:45, Wed., Fri., Sat. 10–9. Planetarium admission: $3.75 adults,*

American Museum of Natural History, **4**

Cathedral of St. John the Divine, **10**

Columbia University, **11**

Columbus Circle, **1**

The Dakota, **2**

Grant's Tomb, **13**

Hayden Planetarium, **4**

Lincoln Center, **5**

Museum of American Folk Art, **6**

New York Historical Society, **3**

Riverside Church, **12**

Soldiers and Sailors Monument, **8**

Symphony Space, **9**

Verdi Square, **7**

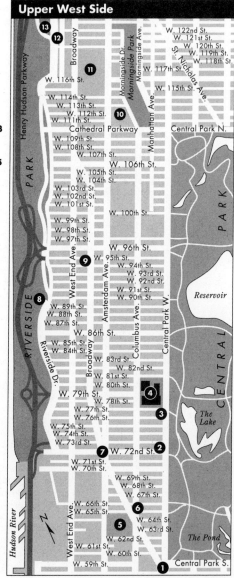

Upper West Side

$2.75 students and senior citizens, $2 children. Call 212/769–5920 for show times.

Upper Broadway Another Upper West Side trail angles diagonally from Columbus Circle up Broadway. At the world headquarters of the **American Bible Society** (1865 Broadway at 61st St.), you ascend a ruby-red carpet to a little-known second-floor museum that has temporary exhibits of the society's worldwide Bible-distributing activities and permanent displays of Helen Keller's 10-volume Braille Bible, a replica of the original Gutenberg press, and a Torah (Jewish scriptures) from China. An adjunct to Lincoln Center, **The Ballet Shop** (1887 Broadway at 62nd St.) sells books and records, photos, paraphernalia, and mementos.

5 Covering an eight-block area west of Broadway between 62nd and 66th streets, **Lincoln Center** is an architecturally unified development that encompasses New York's major-league performing arts institutions. Built during the 1960s to supplant a rundown urban ghetto, the complex can at one time seat nearly 15,000 spectators for performances of classical music, opera, ballet, drama, and film.

Lincoln Center consists of eight distinct units. **Avery Fisher Hall,** named after the founder of Fisher Radio, hosts the New York Philharmonic Orchestra. The Metropolitan Opera and American Ballet Theatre perform at the **Metropolitan Opera House.** The **New York State Theater** is home to the New York City Ballet and the New York City Opera. The **Guggenheim Bandshell,** south of the Met, has free open-air concerts in summer. A single structure devoted to drama includes the **Vivian Beaumont** and **Mitzi E. Newhouse** theaters. The **Library and Museum of the Performing Arts** maintains an extensive collection of records, scores, and books on music, theater, and dance. Across 65th Street lies the world-renowned **Juilliard School,** which houses **Alice Tully Hall,** home of the Chamber Music Society of Lincoln Center, the Film Society of Lincoln Center, and the New York Film Center.

Visitors can wander freely through the lobbies of all buildings and relax in Damrosch Park or beside Lincoln Center's fountains; an outdoor cafe operates throughout the summer. The best free indoor attractions are found in the Performing Arts Library, where visitors can listen to a collection of 42,000 records and tapes or check out any of four galleries. A one-hour guided "Take-the-Tour" covers all the grand theaters. *Tel. 212/877–1800, ext. 512, for schedule. Admission: $6.25 adults, $5.25 students and seniors, $3.50 children.*

Tickets for Lincoln Center events are costly and, because many performances sell out to season subscribers, sometimes impossible to obtain at box offices or through ticket services. Some tickets are usually available just outside the theater during the half-hour before the performance, someone's companion(s) having been unable to make it. Occasionally there are scalpers, and although it's illegal in New York to sell tickets for more than a specified amount above the printed price, such commerce transpires more or less openly before every performance.

6 Across the busy intersection from Lincoln Center, the long-orphaned **Museum of American Folk Art** has found a new home at Columbus Avenue and 66th Street. Its collection includes primitive paintings, quilts, carvings, dolls, trade signs, painted wooden carousel horses, and a giant Indian-chief copper weathervane. *2 Lincoln Sq., tel. 212/977–7175. Admission free. Open daily 9–9.*

Time Out **McGlade's New Pub** (154 Columbus Ave. at 67th St.) is an unpretentious neighborhood joint where you can grab a burger and mingle with the locals, many of whom work on the soaps produced in the ABC studios across the street.

One of the busiest spots on the Upper West Side is the intersection of Broadway, Amsterdam Avenue, and 72nd Street. Officially, the area south of 72nd Street is Sherman Square (for the Union Civil War general, William Tecumseh)
7 and the area north of 72nd Street is **Verdi Square** (for the Italian composer, Giuseppe). Until about a decade ago, Verdi Square was an addicts' hangout known informally as Needle Park. The Upper West Side in general and this intersection in particular have improved consid-

erably in recent years, and real estate values have had a dramatic upsurge.

The subway kiosk on the island south of 72nd Street is an official city landmark, a structure with rounded neo-Dutch moldings that was the first express station north of 42nd Street. Occupying the southeast corner of Amsterdam Avenue and 72nd Street is **Gray's Papaya,** a New York quasi-institution that pairs the sacred (health-enriching papaya and other natural juices) with the profane (hot dogs, smothered in sauerkraut and onions if desired).

Farther up Broadway are two of New York's great food shrines. The fresh produce in the bountiful but unpretentious **Fairway Market** (2127 Broadway at 74th St.) literally bursts onto the street. Have a look at the handmade signs describing the produce and cheese; they can be as fresh as the merchandise itself. At Broadway and 80th Street, **Zabar's** sells exquisite delicatessen items, prepared foods, gourmet groceries, coffees, and cheeses. A mezzanine level has cookware, dishes, and small appliances. The prices are competitive.

When the **Ansonia Hotel** opened at Broadway and 73rd Street in 1904, its white facade, fairy-castle turrets, and new soundproof partitions attracted show people and writers to a hitherto unfashionable area. Now an apartment building, the Ansonia has provided temporary homes for Florenz Ziegfeld, Mischa Elman, Theodore Dreiser, and the great Babe Ruth.

❽ For a quick off-Broadway experience, walk two blocks west to the **Soldiers and Sailors Monument** at Riverside Drive and 89th Street. The monument commemorates Civil War casualties; the environs afford a refreshing view of Riverside Park, the lazy Hudson River, and the New Jersey shore.

Pomander Walk is an attractive slice of Old England wedged between 94th and 95th streets, between Broadway and West End Avenue. The charming enclave was inspired by the stage sets of an American version of a British play of 1911, *Pomander Walk*. Walk in—or peep through the gate if it's locked—and see Tudor houses, win-

dow boxes, and neatly trimmed hedges. Around
the corner, **Symphony Space,** a not-for-profit,
community-sponsored center for the performing
arts, presents a regular schedule of low-priced
(free–$20) classical, international, and contem-
porary concerts, readings, and assorted mara-
thons (Mozart, James Joyce, Cole Porter). *2537
Broadway at 95th St., tel. 212/864–5400.*

The **Cathedral of St. John the Divine,** one block
east of Broadway, is New York's major Episcopal church and the largest Gothic cathedral in
the world (St. Peter's Basilica in Rome is the
only larger church of any kind). The vast 600-
foot nave can seat 5,000 worshipers. Small,
uniquely outfitted chapels border the nave, and
a "Biblical Garden" contains herbs and flowers
mentioned in the Bible. It's still perhaps 100
years from completion, and master craftsmen
are instructing neighborhood youth in the traditional methods of stonecutting and carving.
Along with Sunday services (8, 9, and 11 AM, and
7 PM), the cathedral operates community outreach
programs and presents nonreligious (classical,
folk, winter solstice) concerts. *Amsterdam Ave.
and 112th St., tel. 212/316–7400. Tours Mon.–
Sat. 11, Sun. 12:45.*

The main campus of **Columbia University**
(founded 1754), a large and wealthy private institution, occupies an area bounded by 114th
and 121st streets, Broadway, and Amsterdam
Avenue. Enter from either direction on 116th
Street: The buildings so effectively wall off the
city that it's easy to believe you've been trans-
ported to a more rustic Ivy League campus. The
central campus has the rotunda-topped Low Memorial Library to the north and the massive
Butler Library to the south. A cafe on the southwest corner of the quad has indoor and outdoor
tables perfectly situated for student-watching.

East of the Columbia campus and a short block
farther east of Amsterdam Avenue, Morningside Drive runs along a ridge that lies above
the incline of Morningside Park and affords an
impressive view of the low-rise buildings of
Harlem that stretch across the city.

Riverside Church (Riverside Dr. and 122nd St.,
tel. 212/222–5900) is nondenominational, inter-

racial, international, extremely political, and socially conscious. It is a massive structure with a 356-foot observation tower (admission: $1) and a 74-bell carillon, the largest in the world, whose bells range in weight from 10 pounds to 20 tons. Along with regular Sunday services (10:45 AM), community events, concerts, and dance and theater programs abound. A reasonably priced, reasonably good cafeteria operates on weekdays and Sundays.

Across Riverside Drive, in Riverside Park, stands the General Grant National Memorial Monument, commonly known as **Grant's Tomb,** where the Civil War general and two-term president and his wife rest. In addition to the sarcophagi, the white granite mausoleum contains photographs and Grant memorabilia. *Riverside Dr. and 122nd St., tel. 212/666–1640. Admission free. Open Wed.–Sun. 9–4:30.*

Tour 7. Upper East Side

Numbers in the margin correspond with points of interest on the Upper East Side map.

The Upper East Side is the area east of Central Park between 60th and 96th streets. Long the city's most expensive and desirable residential area, the Upper East Side is the home of old money, new money, foreign money—any kind of money will do. From Fifth Avenue mansions and the smart town houses of the East 60s and 70s to the high-rise corridors of First and Second avenues, this area, more than any other, epitomizes what many people think of as the Manhattan style.

Begin a tour of the Upper East Side at the Plaza. That can mean either **Grand Army Plaza,** an open space along Fifth Avenue between 58th and 60th streets, or the world-famous hotel at the western border of that space. Shaped like the token for a hotel in Monopoly, the **Plaza Hotel** is a registered historical landmark that has been in fashion for upper-crust transients, charity balls, coming-out parties, and romantic rendezvous since 1907.

Grand Army Plaza is flanked by an equestrian statue of William Tecumseh Sherman on the north and the Pulitzer (of Pulitzer Prize fame) Fountain to the south. Appropriately enough for this ritzy area, the fountain is crowned by a female figure representing Abundance. When the fountain is dry (as it is much of the time), its rims become perches for sunbathers and the clients of food vendors who station themselves along the perimeter of the plaza.

Grand Army Plaza, or any intersection along Central Park South, is the place to look for horse-drawn carriage rides. Although most passengers opt for drives through Central Park, technically the carriages can take you almost anywhere you want to go. Like motorized taxi drivers, hansom drivers are independent operators, and the quality of your ride will depend much on their disposition. Carriages operate all year, except in extremely hot or cold weather, and blankets are provided when it's cool. The city sets the official rates ($17 for the first half hour, $5 for each additional 15 minutes), but drivers will often try to get more. Be sure to agree on a price in advance.

Adjacent to Grand Army Plaza stands the **General Motors Building,** an imposing 50-story Georgia marble tower. One section of the main floor lobby displays a dozen or so shining new GM vehicles. The other part of the lobby has recently become the flagship of the legendary **F.A.O. Schwarz** toy store. Bigger than it looks from outside, the toy-o-rama extends up and around the south side of the GM building, all the way over to the Madison Avenue side. A vast selection, good lighting, and gorgeous displays make this a pleasant place to shop—and somewhat compensate for the lofty price tags. The store contains a Hair Parlour for teenage cuts and a Two-Minute Shop where people pressed for time can choose from a selection of wrapped and ready toys.

Central Park Central Park is the 843-acre space bounded by 59th Street and 110th Street, Fifth Avenue and Central Park West (Eighth Avenue). Spared from the schemes of real estate developers by a *New York Evening Post* campaign that began in 1850, Central Park was designed by Frederick

Central Park
Zoo, **5**

Frick
Collection, **7**

Grand Army
Plaza, **1**

Great Lawn, **4**

Guggenheim
Museum, **11**

International
Center of
Photography, **14**

Jewish
Museum, **13**

Loeb
Boathouse, **3**

Metropolitan
Museum of
Art, **10**

El Museo del
Barrio, **16**

Museum of the
City of New
York, **15**

National
Academy of
Design, **12**

Ralph Lauren, **8**

Temple
Emanu-El, **6**

Whitney
Museum, **9**

Wollman Rink, **2**

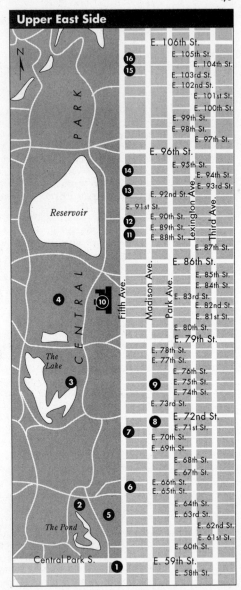

Upper East Side

E. 106th St.
E. 105th St.
E. 104th St.
E. 103rd St.
E. 102nd St.
E. 101st St.
E. 100th St.
E. 99th St.
E. 98th St.
E. 97th St.
E. 96th St.
E. 95th St.
E. 94th St.
E. 93rd St.
E. 92nd St.
E. 91st St.
E. 90th St.
E. 89th St.
E. 88th St.
E. 87th St.
E. 86th St.
E. 85th St.
E. 84th St.
E. 83rd St.
E. 82nd St.
E. 81st St.
E. 80th St.
E. 79th St.
E. 78th St.
E. 77th St.
E. 76th St.
E. 75th St.
E. 74th St.
E. 73rd St.
E. 72nd St.
E. 71st St.
E. 70th St.
E. 69th St.
E. 68th St.
E. 67th St.
E. 66th St.
E. 65th St.
E. 64th St.
E. 63rd St.
E. 62nd St.
E. 61st St.
E. 60th St.
E. 59th St.
E. 58th St.

Central Park S.

PARK

Reservoir

CENTRAL

The
Lake

The Pond

Fifth Ave.
Madison Ave.
Park Ave.
Lexington Ave.
Third Ave.

Law Olmsted and Calvert Vaux and constructed by a crew of 3,000 mainly Irish workmen and 400 horses.

Today Central Park hosts just about any activity a city dweller might engage in out of doors: jogging, cycling, horseback riding, softball, ice skating, croquet, tennis, bird-watching, boating, chess, checkers, theater, concerts, skateboarding, and break dancing. Central Park is reasonably safe during the day and—in populous areas—at night. *Tel. 212/397–3156 for general information, 212/360–1333 for a recorded message on city park events, 212/397–3080 for information on weekend walks and talks led by Urban Park Rangers.*

East Drive is the road that runs north through Central Park from Grand Army Plaza; like West Drive, the southbound artery in the western precincts of the park, it is closed to automobiles on weekends and during some hours on weekdays. Strolling north along East Drive, you soon pass the buildings of the newly renovated Central Park Zoo, which must be entered from the Fifth Avenue side, at 64th Street.

Beyond the zoo, East Drive takes you past the ❷ **Wollman Rink** (tel. 212/517–4800), an iceskating rink that has become a symbol of contemporary urban life. Fruitless and costly attempts by the city to repair the deteriorated facility had kept the rink closed for years, until the builder Donald Trump adopted the project and quickly completed it. In the minds of New Yorkers, the Wollman Rink represents municipal incompetence conquered by the efficiency of private enterprise.

East Drive loops around to **The Mall,** a broad walkway lined with stately elms and busts of famous men. Here one is likely to witness whatever new craze has come along, from the latest dance to some trendy Oriental athletic discipline. The Mall leads to the **Bandshell,** site of summer concerts, speeches, and performance art. A bit farther north, the handsome, newly renovated **Bethesda Fountain** and the graceful iron bridge often model for "Sunday in New York" postcard pictures.

❸ At the **Loeb Boathouse** you can rent a rowboat to cruise the lake or a bike for a spin around the park. You can also buy a fast-food snack or a sit-down lunch. North of the lake is the Ramble, a wooded, hilly area scored by twisting paths, where bird-watchers gather early in the morning, especially during the migratory seasons.

As East Drive moves into the 80s, it passes between the sprawling Metropolitan Museum of Art (on the right) and the eastern edge of the **❹** **Great Lawn** (about 50 yards to the left). The athletic fields of the Great Lawn are busy most summer evenings and on weekends, and its wide expanse has accommodated tens of thousands of people for megaconcerts by Luciano Pavarotti, Diana Ross, Simon and Garfunkel, and others. Should you see a few hundred people picnicking on the ground in an orderly formation that extends around the oval edge of the lawn, you'll know it's summer and there's a performance that night at the nearby **Delacorte Theater** of the New York Shakespeare Festival. *Tel. 212/598–7100. Admission free. Tickets distributed at 6:15 PM for the performance at 8 PM.*

Fifth Avenue Upper Fifth Avenue was settled during the last decade of the 19th century by millionaire migrants from the 34th Street area, the Astors, the Carnegies, the Vanderbilts, and the Whitneys, who moved into palatial stone mansions overlooking newly fashionable Central Park. Few of the residential mansions remain. Some were supplanted by high-rise apartments, others were transformed into museums or foundation headquarters. The west side of Fifth Avenue is one of the few city walks where intersections will not constantly interrupt your stroll.

Fifth Avenue above Grand Army Plaza begins on a literary note, with **open-air bookstalls** operated (when the weather is reasonably clement) by the Strand and Rogers & Cogswell bookstores. The stalls sell new and used books, New York maps and reference material, cassette tapes, and postcards. The best buys are the half-price "reviewers copies" of lightly used recent hardcover books and brand new trade paperbacks.

A few blocks north, at 64th Street, the **Arsenal Building** stands before the entrance to New York City's newest attraction, the 5.5-acre **Central Park Zoo.** Reopened in August 1988 following a five-year, $35 million renovation, the wildlife showcase re-creates a series of habitats that include polar, temperate, and tropical climate zones in which animals roam at will. Visitors look on from various vantage points in each habitat and can even watch the animals' underwater activities. Polar bears and penguins are among the attractions; there are no elephants here. Admission to the adjacent children's zoo is granted to adults only when accompanied by a child. *Central Park at E. 64th St., tel. 212/439–6500. Admission: $1 adults, 25¢ children 3–12, 50¢ senior citizens. Open Apr.–Oct., weekdays 10–5 (May–Sept., Tues. 10–8) weekends and holidays 10–5:30; Nov.–Mar., daily 10–5.*

6 With seats for 2,500 worshippers, **Temple Emanu-el** (1929) is the world's largest Reform Jewish synagogue. The ceiling, marble columns, and great arch of this eclectic limestone structure are covered with mosaics reminiscent of Middle Eastern basilicas. *Fifth Ave. and 65th St., tel. 212/744–1400. Services Mon.–Thurs. 5:30 PM; Fri. 5:15 PM; Sat. 10:30 AM. Guided tours by appointment only.*

7 The **Frick Collection** is housed in the mansion built by the Pittsburgh coke and steel baron Henry Clay Frick. It was designed to display his private collection of art, and a bona fide masterpiece graces almost every room: Renoir's *Mother and Children*, Rembrandt's *Self-Portrait*, Fragonard's *The Progress of Love*, and distinguished works by Bellini, Vermeer, Titian, El Greco, Turner, Whistler, and Gainsborough. Even the rest area is a masterpiece: a tranquil indoor court with a fountain and glass ceiling. *1 E. 70th St., tel. 212/288–0700. Admission: $3 adults, $1.50 students and seniors. Open Tues.–Sat. 10–6, Sun. and holidays 1–6.*

The Madison Mile Just before World War I, the railroad tracks down the center of Park Avenue were covered with a roadway, and Park Avenue, like Fifth

Avenue, became a distinguished residential thoroughfare. Between the two avenues, the low-rise brownstones of Madison Avenue, which had started out as a commercial universe serving the grand mansions of Fifth Avenue, remain unchanged.

The connotation of "Madison Avenue" has undergone a major change in recent years. New Yorkers no longer readily associate the words (or the place) with the advertising business, much of which has fled Madison Avenue in the East 40s and 50s for less costly downtown real estate. Madison Avenue, in particular the Madison Mile between 59th and 79th streets, is now the home of high chic: The lower stories of Madison Avenue's brownstones house many of the world's major fashion designers, patrician art galleries, and unique specialty stores. For the most part, these shops are small, intimate, expensive, and almost invariably closed on Sunday.

Heading uptown and working both sides of the street, you come to **The Gazebo** (660 Madison Ave.) with country-style home furnishings such as quilts, pottery, wicker work, and rag rugs. **The Coach Store** (710 Madison Ave.) devotes two floors to fine leather. **M. J. Knoud** (716 Madison Ave.) purveys hunting and polo saddles and accessories, jockey silks, and other equine-themed clothing and gear.

As opulent as the boudoirs for which its wares are destined, **La Lingerie** (792 Madison Ave.) features high-priced nightgowns, dressing gowns, embroidered shawls, and other intimate apparel. At the same address, **Sonia Rykiel** sells expensive high-fashion garments in styles that won't go out of style next month.

Owned by the sometime New York Yankees manager, **Billy Martin's Western Wear** (812 Madison Ave.) features urbane renderings of city-slicker saddlebags, cowboy shirts, suede jackets, Indian-style silver, beaded jewelry, and snakeskin-brimmed baseball caps for all the major league teams. A familiar name in European high fashion, **Giorgio Armani** (815 Madison Ave.) is a "soft-tech" setting for men's and women's clothing in Armani-made and licensed lines. One of the first Madison Mile designer boutiques, **St. Laurent Rive-Gauche** (855 Madison Ave.) is a somewhat haughty place to shop for women's fashions, accessories, and cosmetics.

8 By far the most spectacular store on Madison Mile, **Ralph Lauren** (867 Madison Ave.) hardly seems like a store at all. In fact, it's the landmark Rhinelander Mansion replete with walnut fittings, oriental carpets, family portraits, and all that high-style preppie clothing that seems to be lying around waiting to be put away. The atmosphere surpasses unintimidating; it's actually inviting. Be sure to visit the fourth-floor home furnishings section, where merchandise is arrayed in to-the-manor-born dream suites.

One Night Stand (905 Madison Ave., tel. 212/772–7720) *rents* designer ball gowns and cocktail dresses; call for an appointment. **Antiquarian** (948 Madison Ave.) is a small gallery that specializes in fine ancient art.

Time Out In a neighborhood where reasonably priced eating spots are scarce, **Soup Burg** (922 Madison Ave.) is a clean, well-lighted coffee shop that dishes up burgers and soup, salads, all sorts of sandwiches, and breakfast (featuring home-(made oatmeal) any time of day.

9 The **Whitney Museum of American Art** is a gray granite vault separated from Madison Avenue materialism by a dry moat. An outgrowth of a gallery that began in the studio of the sculptor and collector Gertrude Vanderbilt Whitney, the museum is devoted exclusively to 20th-century American work, from naturalism and impressionism to pop art, abstractionism, and whatever comes next. *945 Madison Ave. at 75th St., tel. 212/570–3676. Admission: $4.50 adults, $2.50 seniors; free for students and children at all times and for everyone Tues. 6–8. Open Tues. 1–8; Wed.–Sat. 11–5; Sun. noon–6.*

Just off Madison is the so-called **Gucci Townhouse** (16 E. 76th St.), the former Gucci family mansion, which in 1988 sold for $7 million, at the time the most ever paid for a New York town house.

Continue north on Madison to the **Frank E. Campbell Funeral Chapel** (1076 Madison Ave. at 81st St.), *the* place for fashionable funerals since 1898. The somber chocolate-color edifice has seen massive funeral events for Rudolph Valentino (1926) and Judy Garland (1969) and more recent ceremonies for Robert Kennedy, John Lennon, and Rita Hayworth. Across the street you may recognize P.S. 6 as Justin Henry's school in *Kramer v. Kramer*.

Museum Mile Museum Mile is a strip of cultural institutions located on or near Fifth Avenue between 82nd and 104th streets. Although the structures themselves and their contents represent a broad spectrum of subjects and styles, most of them have at least two things in common: They are closed Monday, and they allow free admission on Tuesday evening.

❿ The **Metropolitan Museum of Art** has valid evidence for billing itself "New York's number one tourist attraction." This is the largest art museum in the Western Hemisphere (1.6 million square feet), and its permanent collection of 3.3 million works of art includes items from prehistoric to modern times from all areas of the world. Its 19 curatorial departments include the world's most comprehensive collection of American art, and its holdings of European art are unequaled outside Europe. The museum also has one of the world's best collections of ancient Greek, Roman, and Egyptian art.

Within this "city of art," we tend to prefer the old neighborhoods. The small chamber lined with reliefs from the Northwest Palace of the Assyrian King Assurnasirpal II (BC 882–859) replicates the serene atmosphere of an undiscovered tomb. The Astor Court Chinese garden reproduces a Ming Dynasty (1368–1644) scholar's courtyard with water splashing over artfully positioned rocks. The magnificent Temple of Dendur (circa BC 15) was transplanted from Egypt to a huge gallery with a wall of windows looking onto Central Park.

Walking tours and lectures are free with your admission contribution. Tours covering various sections of the museum begin about every 15 minutes on weekdays, less frequently on weekends.

They depart from the Tour Board in the Great Hall (main entrance), but you may attach yourself to any group you encounter along the way. Lectures, which are often related to temporary exhibits, are given on Sunday, Tuesday, and Friday. *Fifth Ave. at 82nd St., tel. 212/535–7710. Suggested contribution: $5 adults, $2.50 seniors and students, children free. Open Tues. 9:30–8:45, Wed.–Sun. 9:30–5:15.*

❶ An inverted concrete cone, Frank Lloyd Wright's **Guggenheim Museum** is a six-story corkscrew through which you wind down past mobiles, stabiles, and other exemplars of modern art. Displays alternate new artists and modern masters; the permanent collection includes more than 20 Picassos. *1071 Fifth Ave. at 89th St., tel. 212/360–3500. Admission: $4.50 adults, $2.50 students and seniors, free Tues. 5–7:45. Open Tues. 11–7:45, Wed.–Sun. 11–4:45.*

❷ Housed in a stately 19th-century mansion, the exhibits of **The National Academy of Design** usually focus on comparatively unsung artists of Europe and America. *1083 Fifth Ave. at 89th St., tel. 212/369–4880. Admission: $2.50 adults, $2 seniors and students, free Tues. 5–8. Open Tues. noon–8, Wed.–Sun. noon–5.*

A former residence of the industrialist and philanthropist Andrew Carnegie now houses the **Cooper-Hewitt Museum,** officially the Smithsonian Institution's National Museum of Design. Exhibitions, which change regularly, focus on an aspect of contemporary or historical design. Major holdings include: drawings, prints, textiles, furniture, metalwork, ceramics, glass, woodwork, and wall coverings. *2 E. 91st St., tel. 212/860–6868. Admission: $3 adults, $1.50 seniors and students, free Tues. 5–9. Open Tues. 10–9, Wed.–Sat. 10–5, Sun. noon–5.*

Time Out **Jackson Hole** (Madison Ave. at 91st St.) is a cheerful spot that serves the great American hamburger, sandwiches, omelets, chicken, and salads. Ski posters evoke the mood of the eponymous Wyoming resort. Prices are reasonable; beer and wine are available.

13 The largest collection of Jewish ceremonial objects in the Western Hemisphere is housed in the **Jewish Museum.** The gift shop offers a wide selection of Jewish books and memorabilia. *1109 Fifth Ave. at 92nd St., tel. 212/860–1888. Admission: $4 adults, $2 seniors and students, free Tues. 5–8. Open Sun. 11–6, Mon., Wed., Thurs. noon–5, Tues. noon–8.*

14 Located in a landmark mansion at the corner of Fifth Avenue and 94th Street, the **International Center of Photography** (ICP) generally focuses its exhibits on the work of a single prominent photographer or one photographic genre (portraits, architecture, holography). The bookstore carries an impressive array of photography-oriented books, prints, and postcards; courses and special programs are offered throughout the year. *1130 Fifth Ave., tel. 212/860–1777. Admission: $3 adults, $1 seniors, $1.50 students, $1 children under 12, free Tues. 5–8. Open Tues. noon–8, Wed.–Fri. noon–5, Sat.–Sun. 11–6.*

15 The **Museum of the City of New York** makes the history of the Big Apple—from the Dutch settlers of Nieuw Amsterdam to yesterday's headlines—come to life with period rooms, dioramas, slide shows, and clever displays of memorabilia. Weekend programs appeal especially to children. *Fifth Ave. at 103rd St., tel. 212/534–1672. Suggested contribution: $3 adults, $1.50 students and seniors, $1 children. Open Tues.–Sat. 10–5; Sun. and holidays, 1–5.*

16 The final stop on Museum Mile, **El Museo del Barrio,** concentrates on Latin culture in general, with a particular emphasis on Puerto Rican art. The permanent collection includes numerous pre-Columbian artifacts. *1230 Fifth Ave. at 104th St., tel. 212/831–7272. Suggested contribution, $2. Open Wed.–Sun. 11–5.*

Tour 8. Greenwich Village

Numbers in the margin correspond with points of interest on the Greenwich Village map.

Writers and artists have converged on Greenwich Village for generations. In the 19th century the writers Henry James, Edgar Allan

Poe, Mark Twain, Walt Whitman, and Stephen
Crane lived and worked in the area. The turn of
the century brought O. Henry, Edith Wharton,
Theodore Dreiser, and Hart Crane. During the
1920s and 1930s, John Dos Passos, Norman
Rockwell, Sinclair Lewis, Eugene O'Neill, Edward Hopper, and Edna St. Vincent Millay
resided in its row houses and frequented its
speakeasies.

During the late 1940s and early 1950s, Village
cultural life was dominated by the abstract expressionist painters Franz Kline, Jackson
Pollock, Mark Rothko, and Willem de Kooning
and the beat writers Jack Kerouac, Allen Ginsberg, and Lawrence Ferlinghetti. A later wave
brought the folk musicians and poets of the
1960s, led by Bob Dylan and Peter, Paul, and
Mary.

As in much of Manhattan, high rents have priced
all but the most affluent out of the Greenwich
Village housing market. Today the Village—
New Yorkers almost invariably speak of it simply as "the Village"—is inhabited principally by
affluent professionals, students, and others as-
piring to blend the flavor of small-town life with
the bright lights of the big city.

❶ Begin a tour of Greenwich Village at Washington Arch in **Washington Square** at the foot of
Fifth Avenue. Designed by Stanford White,
Washington Arch was built in 1892 to commemorate the 100th anniversary of George Washington's presidential inauguration and was originally placed about half a block north of its
present location. The permanent arch was built
in 1906 and the statues—*Washington at War* on
the left, *Washington at Peace* on the right—
were added in 1913. The body builder Charles
Atlas modeled for *Peace*.

Washington Square started out as a cemetery,
principally for yellow fever victims, and an estimated 10,000–22,000 bodies lie below. In the
early 1800s it was a parade ground and the site
of public executions; bodies dangled from a conspicuous Hanging Elm at the northwest corner
of the Square. Later it became the focus of a
fashionable residential neighborhood and the
center of outdoor activity.

By the early 1980s, Washington Square had deteriorated into a tawdry place only a drug dealer could love. Then community activism motivated a police crackdown that sent the drug traffic elsewhere and made Washington Square comfortable again for frisbee players, street musicians, skateboarders, jugglers, stand-up comics, sitters, strollers, and the twice-a-year art fair.

Most of the buildings bordering Washington Square belong to New York University. "The Row" of federal town houses along Washington Square North, between Fifth Avenue and University Place, serves as faculty housing. The house at **20 Washington Square North** is the oldest building (1820) on the block. You can tell it was built before 1830 by the Flemish bond brickwork—alternate bricks inserted with the smaller surface facing out. Before 1830, builders thought that this was the only way to build walls that would stand.

Turn north on MacDougal Street and walk a half-block to **MacDougal Alley,** a private (fenced with locked gate) cobblestone street where stables and carriage houses have been converted into charming homes adorned with gas lamps.

Eighth Street, the main commercial strip of the Village, is not the "real" Greenwich Village but a collection of fast-food purveyors, poster and record shops, and glitzy clothing stores whose customers are chiefly the "bridge and tunnel people"—a disparaging term that Manhattan dwellers assign to those who come to the city from the other boroughs or the suburbs.

For a more authentic village atmosphere, go north on Sixth Avenue to **Balducci's** (Sixth Ave. and 9th St.), a full-service gourmet department store that sprouted from the vegetable stand of the late Louis Balducci, Sr. Along with more than 80 Italian cheeses and 50 kinds of bread, this family-owned enterprise features imported Italian specialties and a prodigious selection of fresh seafood.

Directly opposite, the triangle formed by West 10th Street, Sixth Avenue, and Greenwich Avenue originally held a greenmarket, a jail, and

❷ the magnificent courthouse that is now the **Jefferson Market Library.** Critics termed the courthouse's hodgepodge of styles Venetian, Victorian, or Italian; Villagers, noting the alternating wide bands of red brick and narrow strips of granite, dubbed it Lean Bacon style. Over the years the structure has housed a number of government agencies (public works, civil defense, census bureau, police academy) but was on the verge of demolition when public-spirited citizens saved it and turned it into a public library in 1967. Note the fountain at the corner of West 10th Street and Sixth Avenue and the seal of the City of New York on the east front; on the inside, look at the handsome interior doorways and climb the graceful circular stairway.

Time Out   Greenwich Village boasts a multitude of trendy places that brew cappuccino, yet only a few of them are true coffeehouses. **Gran Caffe Degli Artisti** (46 Greenwich Ave.) is the real thing, complete with mismatched thrift shop furniture, modern paintings and ancient artifacts clinging to bare brick walls, a bulletin board of neighborhood happenings, and bohemian patrons. In addition to ambitious permutations of coffee, the menu includes sandwiches, salads, pastries, and American and Italian soft drinks.

Take Christopher Street, which veers off from the southern end of the library triangle, a few steps to **Gay Street.** A bending lane lined with small row houses circa 1810, Gay Street was originally a black neighborhood and later a strip of speakeasies. Ruth McKinney lived and wrote *My Sister Eileen* in the basement of No. 14, and Howdy Doody was designed in the basement of No. 12.

Go west on Christopher past the **Lion's Head** (59 Christopher St.), a longtime hangout for literati.

❸ At **Sheridan Square,** Christopher Street becomes the heart of New York's gay community and the location of many intriguing boutiques.

West of Seventh Avenue, the Village turns into a picture-book town of twisting, tree-lined

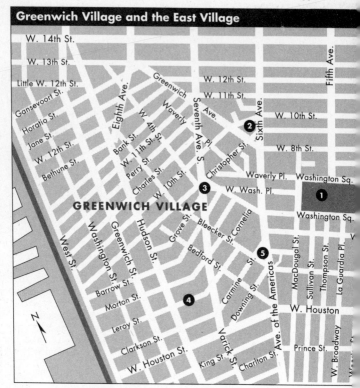

Greenwich Village and the East Village

W. 14th St.

W. 13th St.

Little W. 12th St.

Gansevoort St.

Horatio St.

Jane St.

W. 12th St.

Bethune St.

Greenwich Ave.

W. 12th St.

W. 11th St.

Eighth Ave.

Waverly Pl.

W. 4th St.

Bank St.

W. 11th St.

Perry St.

Charles St.

W. 10th St.

Seventh Ave. S.

Christopher St.

Sixth Ave.

Fifth Ave.

W. 10th St.

W. 8th St.

Waverly Pl.

Washington Sq.

W. Wash. Pl.

Washington Sq.

GREENWICH VILLAGE

Washington St.

Greenwich St.

Hudson St.

Grove St.

Bleecker St.

Cornelia St.

Bedford St.

Carmine St.

Downing St.

Ave. of the Americas

MacDougal St.

Sullivan St.

Thompson St.

La Guardia Pl.

West St.

Barrow St.

Morton St.

Leroy St.

Clarkson St.

W. Houston St.

Varick St.

King St.

Charlton St.

W. Houston

Prince St.

W. Broadway

N

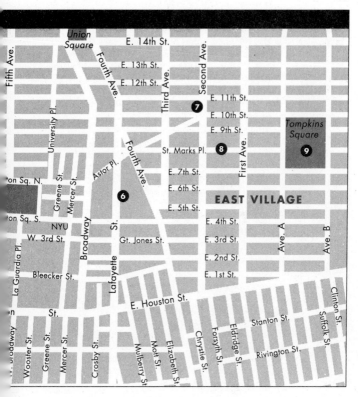

Union Square

Fifth Ave.

E. 14th St.

E. 13th St.

Fourth Ave.

E. 12th St.

Third Ave.

Second Ave.

E. 11th St.

❼

E. 10th St.

E. 9th St.

University Pl.

Astor Pl.

Fourth Ave.

St. Marks Pl.

❽

First Ave.

Tompkins Square

❾

Greene St.

Mercer St.

E. 7th St.

E. 6th St.

E. 5th St.

EAST VILLAGE

on Sq. N.

Broadway

St.

❻

on Sq. S.

NYU

E. 4th St.

W. 3rd St.

Lafayette

Gt. Jones St.

E. 3rd St.

E. 2nd St.

Ave. A

Ave. B

La Guardia Pl.

Bleecker St.

E. 1st St.

n St.

E. Houston St.

Clinton St.

oadway

Wooster St.

Greene St.

Mercer St.

Crosby St.

Mulberry St.

Elizabeth St.

Mott St.

Chrystie St.

Forsyth St.

Eldridge St.

Stanton St.

Suffolk St.

Rivington St.

streets, quaint houses, and tiny restaurants. Follow Grove Street from Sheridan Square past the boyhood home of the poet Hart Crane (45 Grove St.) to the house at the corner of Grove and Bedford streets. This building merits notice as one of the few clapboard structures in the Village; wood construction was banned as a fire hazard in 1822, the year it was built. The house has served many functions; it housed a brothel during the Civil War.

Grove Street curves before the iron gate of **Grove Court,** an enclave of brick-fronted town houses of the middle 1800s. Built originally as apartments for employees at neighborhood hotels, Grove Court was called Mixed Ale Alley because of the residents' propensity to pool beverages brought from work. It now houses a more affluent crowd: A town house there recently sold for $3 million.

Time Out An unmarked doorway on the west side of Bedford Street between Grove and Barrow leads to good food, strong drink, and loads of local color. Opened as a speakeasy in the 1920s, **Chumley's** (86 Bedford St. at Barrow St., tel. 212/675–4449) became a hangout for the writers John Steinbeck, John Dos Passos, and Ring Lardner. Also accessible through an arched doorway around the corner on Barrow Street, Chumley's features burgers, English-style specials, and a popular weekend brunch.

The building at 77 Bedford Street is the oldest house in the Village (1799), yet the place next door has a greater claim to fame. Not only was 75½ Bedford the residence (at different times) of Edna St. Vincent Millay and John Barrymore, it is also New York's narrowest house. Just 9½ feet wide, the lot was an alley until rising real estate prices inspired the construction.

Heading west on Commerce Street, you soon reach the **Cherry Lane Theater,** one of the original Off-Broadway houses and the site of American premieres of works by O'Neill, Beckett, Ionesco, and Albee. Across the street stand two identical brick houses separated by a garden. Popularly known as the **Twin Sisters,** the houses were built (according to legend) by a sea captain for two daughters who loathed one another. Historical record insists they were built by a milkman who needed the two houses and an open courtyard for his work.

Barrow and Hudson streets meet at the corner of a block owned by **St. Luke's-in-the-Fields,** a simple country church whose grounds are made available to church members and neighborhood residents for gardening space.

❹ Head south on Hudson Street to **St. Luke's Place,** a row of classic town houses of the 1860s, shaded by graceful ginkgo trees. Mayor Jimmy Walker lived at No. 6. The lampposts are "mayor's lamps," which were sometimes placed in front of the residences of New York mayors. Theodore Dreiser wrote *An American Tragedy* at No. 16. No. 12 is the residence of the Huxtable family depicted in the credits of *The Cosby Show*—but the Huxtables purportedly live in Brooklyn. Before 1890 the playground on the south side of St. Luke's Place was a graveyard where, according to legend, the dauphin of France, the lost son of Louis XVI and Marie Antoinette, is interred.

Across Seventh Avenue, St. Luke's Place becomes Leroy Street, which terminates in an old Italian neighborhood at Bleecker Street. Amazingly unchanged amid all the Village gentrification, Bleecker between Sixth and Seventh avenues abounds with fragrant Italian bakeries (**Zitos,** 259 Bleecker St.), butcher shops (**Ottomanelli's,** 285 Bleecker St.), pastry shops, fish stores, vegetable markets, pizza stands, and restaurants. The activity here focuses on **Father Demo Square** (Bleecker St. and Sixth Ave.), once a cluster of pushcarts and now the site of the **Church of Our Lady of Pompei,** where St. Francis Xavier Cabrini, the first American saint, often prayed.

Across Sixth Avenue lies the stretch of Bleecker Street depicted in songs by Bob Dylan and other folk singers of the 1960s. Standing in the shadow of New York University, the area around the intersection of Bleecker and MacDougal streets attracts a young crowd to its cafes, bars, jazz clubs, coffeehouses, pizza stands, Off-Broadway theaters (**Provincetown Playhouse, Minetta**

Lane Theater), cabarets **(Village Gate),** fast-food stands, and unpretentious restaurants.

Continuing north on MacDougal, you pass two houses (127 MacDougal St. and 129 MacDougal St.) once owned by Aaron Burr, who held much of the land that became Greenwich Village. At the end of the block, you've returned to Washington Square.

Tour 9. The East Village

The gritty tenements of the East Village—an area bounded by 14th Street on the north, Fourth Avenue or the Bowery on the west, Houston Street on the south, and the East River —provided inexpensive living places for artists, writers, and actors until very recently. Now the East Village is as costly a place to live as anywhere else south of 96th Street. Yet, in a way, the area has the best of both worlds. The new residents have been accompanied by new restaurants, shops, and galleries, while the old East Villagers maintain the fascinating trappings of the counterculture.

To explore the East Village, begin at the intersection of East 8th Street, Fourth Avenue, and Astor Place. Works of modern sculpture occupy two traffic islands in the square: One island contains *Alamo*, a massive black cube sculpted by Bernard Rosenthal; another island bears an ornate Beaux Arts subway entrance that provides access to the uptown #6 trains. Weather permitting, the sidewalks on the southern edge of Astor Place become a makeshift flea market.

On one corner of the intersection stands **Astor Wine and Spirits** (12 Astor Pl.), one of New York's most comprehensive and attractive liquor stores. It has good prices on imports, even better deals on house brands. (New York State has unexpectedly restrictive liquor control laws: Liquor and wine can be sold only in liquor stores, which can sell *only* liquor and wine—no beer, soda, ice, or glasses—and must close on Sunday.)

Continue west on Astor Place to **Astor Place Hair Designers** (2 Astor Pl.), where lines stretch out to the sidewalk awaiting service by four levels of barbers. Choose your cut from Polaroid snapshots in the window—maybe a Village Cut, a Guido, or a Li'l Tony. It costs only $10 for men and $12 for ladies, and it's open every day.

Returning to Fourth Avenue and heading south on Lafayette Street, you quickly come upon **Colonnade Row.** These run-down row houses of 1833, fronted by marble Corinthian columns, were once inhabited by John Jacob Astor and Cornelius Vanderbilt.

In 1854 Astor opened the city's first free library in the imposing structure directly across the street. That building now houses a significant New York institution, the New York Shakespeare Festival's **Public Theater.** The Public's six playhouses (and a cinema) present plays from abroad, some classic theater, and challenging new work by young American writers. *A Chorus Line* had its first performances here. The New York Shakespeare Festival is in the midst of a six-year Shakespeare marathon that, for the first time in America, will present all 37 plays consecutively. *425 Lafayette St., tel. 212/598–7150. Theater tickets: $25 for regular performances, $30 for Shakespeare marathon productions. Some half-price tickets for most performances available at 6 PM (matinees, 1 PM); the line forms 1–2 hrs earlier.*

Cooper Square takes its name from Peter Cooper, an industrialist who in 1859 founded a college to provide a forum for public opinion and free technical education for the working class. The brownstone **Cooper Union Foundation Building** at Astor Place and Fourth Avenue was the first structure to be supported by steel railroad rails—rolled in Cooper's own plant. Cooper Union still offers tuition-free education and an active public affairs program. A basement art gallery presents changing exhibits on history and design.

Old New York joke: Q. How do you get to Carnegie Hall? A. Practice, practice, practice. Variation on old New York joke: Q. How do you get to Carnegie Hall? A. Go to the **Carl Fischer Music Store** (62 Cooper Sq., tel. 212/677–1148), select from the infinitude of sheet music, confer with the knowledgeable staff, mingle with the other musicians hanging out, and practice, practice, practice.

You will probably find **McSorley's Old Ale House** (15 E. 7th St.), one of several claimants to the distinction of being New York's oldest bar, crammed with college types enticed by McSorley's own brands of ale. It opened in 1854 and did not admit women until 1970.

Surma, The Ukrainian Shop (11 E. 7th St.) reminds you that the East Village is essentially a Ukrainian neighborhood of onion-domed churches, butcher shops, bakeries, and restaurants serving hearty Middle European fare. What does a Ukrainian shop carry? Ukrainian books, magazines, and cassette tapes; greeting cards; musical instruments; colorful painted eggs and Surma's own brand of egg coloring; honey; and an exhaustive selection of peasant blouses.

Stuyvesant Street veers away from St. Marks Place and Third Avenue at an angle and runs through what was once Governor Peter Stuyvesant's "bouwerie," or farm. The street ends before **St. Mark's Church-in-the-Bowery,** a fieldstone country church of 1799 appended with a Greek Revival steeple and cast-iron front porch. Stuyvesant and Commodore Perry are buried in the cemetery beside the city's oldest continually used church, which has hosted much countercultural activity over the years. In the 1920s a forward-thinking pastor injected the Episcopalian ritual with American Indian chants, Greek folk dancing, and Eastern mantras. During the hippie era, St. Mark's welcomed avant-garde poets and playwrights. Today, dancers, poets, and performance artists cavort in the main sanctuary, where pews have been removed to accommodate them.

Second Avenue borders the church on the east, a thoroughfare that in the early part of this century was known as the Yiddish Rialto. Between Houston and 14th streets, eight theaters presented Yiddish-language productions of musicals, revues, and heart-wrenching melodramas. Today the theaters are gone; all that remains are Hollywood-style stars (Stars of David, that is) embedded in the sidewalk in front of the **Second Avenue Deli** (Second Ave. and 10th St.) to commemorate the Yiddish stage luminaries.

Time Out **Veselka** (144 Second Ave. at 9th St.) is a down-home neighborhood hangout that serves hearty soups, overstuffed sandwiches, and solid Ukrainian and Polish specialties such as blintzes, pirogi, and boiled beef with horseradish. The decor is classic 1950s luncheonette, highlighted with murals of East Village life.

❽ The intersection of Second Avenue and **St. Marks Place** (the name given to 8th Street in the East Village) is the hub of the "hip" East Village. During the 1950s Allen Ginsberg and Jack Kerouac lived and wrote in the area; the 1960s brought Bill Graham's Fillmore East, the Electric Circus, and hallucinogenic drugs to these blocks. The black-clad, pink-haired or shaven-headed punks followed, and many of them remain today. St. Marks Place between Second and Third avenues is a counterculture bazaar lined with vegetarian restaurants, jewelry stalls, leather shops, haircutters, and stores selling books, posters, and weird clothing. If you want to find a souvenir that will shock Aunt Minnie, this is the place to look. The East Village manages to get all the new styles first; the trend that *Time* magazine will discover in six months is parading St. Marks Place today.

East of Second Avenue, the area becomes more arty. **Theater 80** (80 St. Marks Pl., tel. 212/254–7400), one of New York's few remaining revival movie houses, shows a different double feature almost daily (same show Friday and Saturday); the fare includes American and foreign classics, relatively recent films, and cult classics.

P.S. 122 (150 First Ave. at 9th St., tel. 212/477–5288) is a former public school building transformed into a complex of spaces for avant-garde entertainment. Shocking, often crude, and frequently unpredictable, P.S. 122 happenings translate the spirit of the street into performance art. Prices are low, rarely more than $10, except for occasional benefit performances.

➒ Far East Village activities focus on **Tompkins Square,** the park bordered by avenues A and B and 7th and 10th streets. Although the square itself could use a facelift, the restored brownstones along 10th Street are evidence that Tompkins Square is already smartly gentrified.

Not long ago, the outer limits of the East Village were a hotbed of avant-garde activity. More than two dozen art galleries, with names like Gracie Mansion and P.P.O.W., featured work that was often startling, innovative, or political. The art dealers, however, have either gone out of business or moved to more mainstream (and spacious) locations in SoHo or other parts of the Village.

Time Out Mingle with undiscovered artists and refugees from the 1960s at the **Life Cafe** (343 E. 10th St. at Ave. B, tel. 212/477–9001). The name comes from the *Life* magazine photos shellacked onto the walls. The menu is mainly Mexican, augmented with burgers, sandwiches, and vegetarian concoctions. There is outdoor seating when the weather permits—and a full bar.

Tour 10. SoHo

Numbers in the margin correspond with points of interest on the SoHo, Little Italy, and Chinatown map.

Twenty years ago, SoHo (the district *S*outh of *Ho*uston Street, bounded by Broadway, Canal Street, and Sixth Avenue) had just about been left for dead. In 1962 a City Club of New York study called this area of small 19th-century factories and warehouses "the wasteland of New York City" and "commercial slum number one." Numerous industrial fires had earned it the nickname Hell's Hundred Acres.

Two factors changed the perception and the fate of SoHo. One was the discovery that the hot hundred contained the world's greatest concentration of cast-iron buildings. The architectural rage between 1860 and 1890, cast-iron buildings did not require massive walls to bear the weight of the upper stories. Lighter and less expensive than stone, they were produced from standardized molds to mimic any architectural style: Italianate, Victorian Gothic, and neo-Greek can be seen today in SoHo. By eliminating load-bearing walls, cast-iron buildings gained interior space and made possible larger windows. Many subsequent nonmetallic buildings attempted to copy the graceful cast-iron design; how can you tell true cast-iron buildings from the counterfeits? Hold a magnet against the suspect and see whether it sticks.

The other factor of the SoHo renaissance was the influx of artists attracted to the large, cheap, well-lighted spaces that cast-iron buildings provided. At first it was illegal for artists to live in their lofts; then, during the 1970s, the municipal zoning laws were changed to permit residence. However, as the tide of artists and galleries and quaint cafes made this convenient neighborhood a more attractive residential area, the rising rents forced out all but the most successful artists.

Today, SoHo offers architecture and art, high-style shopping, and plenty of intriguing places to eat and drink. West Broadway (which runs parallel to and four blocks west of Broadway) is SoHo's main drag and the location of many shops and galleries. Saturday is the big day for gallery-hopping, and it's when the sidewalks of SoHo turn into a strolling fashion show of today's wildest styles.

South on West Broadway from Houston Street (pronounced "How-ston"), **Circle Gallery** (468 West Broadway) spotlights a number of artists at a time and sells posters and jewelry. **Suzanne Bartsch** (456A West Broadway) is a semi-Oriental setting for British-designed clothing. **Victoria Falls** (451 West Broadway) sells authentic antique and reproduced women's clothing, including fine lingerie and handknit sweaters.

❶ **420 West Broadway** is one address that houses several galleries: **Leo Castelli Gallery** displays the big names of modern art; **Sonnabend Gallery** has important American and European artists; the **49th Parallel** features Canadian artists; and **Charles Cowles Gallery** has fine painting, sculpture, and photography. Several show-

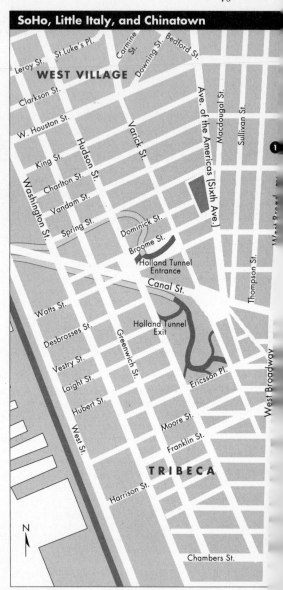

SoHo, Little Italy, and Chinatown

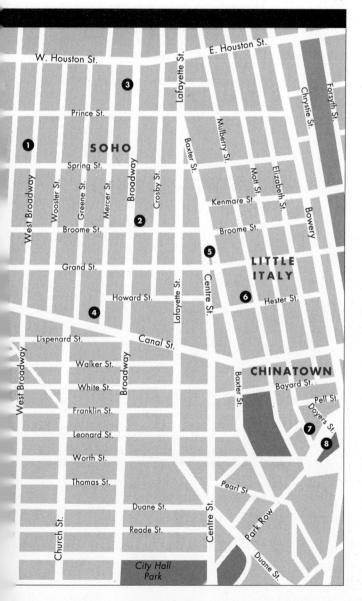

rooms in the **Mary Boone Gallery** (417 West Broadway) display what's hot in contemporary art.

It's hard to overlook **Think Big** (390 West Broadway), a shop that features elephantine versions of sporting goods, items commonly found in the home, and souvenirs. Next door, **D. F. Sanders & Co.** (386 West Broadway) markets contemporary furnishings and housewares that look stylish enough to make housework seem like fun. The **O. K. Harris Gallery** (383 West Broadway) is known for works of photorealism and unusual sculpture.

Time Out   Noisy, often bursting at the seams with young professionals from the Financial District, the **Manhattan Brewing Company** (40–42 Thompson St., tel. 212/219–9250) is a fine place to stop for a quick meal and seven kinds of 100% natural beer. Brewed on the premises (but not in the gleaming copper vats displayed in the Tap Room), the beer is exceptionally fresh and tasty. The food is okay, and reasonably priced: chili, burgers, Irish stew, and such grazing fare as Buffalo wings, fried zucchini, and potato skins.

SoHo's finest cast-iron architecture lies east of West Broadway. Head east on Broome Street and cross Wooster Street, which is paved with Belgian blocks, a smoother successor to the traditional cobblestone. The **Gunther Building,** with its gracefully curving window panes, stands at the southwest corner of Broome and Greene streets. Go north on Greene to #72–76, the so-called **King of Greene Street,** a five-story, Renaissance-style, cast-iron building with a magnificent projecting porch of Corinthian columns. Today the King (now painted yellow) houses three art galleries (**Ariel, Condeso Lawler,** and **M–13**) plus **The Second Coming,** a department store of "vintage"—too old for "secondhand," not old enough for "antique"— women's and men's clothing, furniture, and other curiosities. The **Queen of Greene Street** (28-30 Greene St.) is a Second Empire cast-iron structure with a huge mansard roof but no retail enterprises.

Continue east on Broome Street to the corner of Broome and Broadway to see a classic of the **②** cast-iron genre, the 1857 **Haughwout Building** (488 Broadway). Inspired by a Venetian palace, this five-story blackened Parthenon of Cast Iron contained the world's first commercial passenger elevator, a steam-powered device invented by Elisha Graves Otis. For a closer look at the tin ceilings and interior columns, and perhaps a bargain on linens or underwear, step inside the **Soho Mill Outlet** on the ground floor.

The Broome-Broadway intersection is a few blocks from SoHo's two unusual museums. The **③** **New Museum of Contemporary Art** shows experimental, often radically innovative work by unrecognized artists. It will display nothing more than 10 years old. *583 Broadway between Houston and Prince Sts., tel. 212/219-1355. Suggested admission: $2.50 adults, $1.50 students, seniors, and artists. Open Wed.–Sun. noon–6; Fri.–Sat. noon–8.*

④ The **Museum of Holography** has a permanent exhibit on the history of holograms, three-dimensional photographs created by laser beams. This combination science show and art gallery projects a film on holography and has three changing exhibits a year. The gift shop has a terrific selection of 3-D art and souvenirs. *11 Mercer St. (near Canal St.), tel. 212/925-0581. Admission: $3 adults, $2.75 students, $1.75 children and seniors. Open Tues.–Sun. 11–6.*

Tour 11. Little Italy

Where are the cops when you need them? Certainly not in the former **police headquarters** **⑤** **building,** a magnificent 1909 Renaissance palazzo that occupies the entire block bounded by Grand, Centre, and Broome streets and Centre Market Place. The police moved to new quarters in 1973, and the stately domed edifice has been converted into a luxury co-op project aptly called the **Police Building,** where apartments range in price from $338,500 to $1,746,000.

Walk one block east to Grand and Mulberry streets, and you enter Little Italy. Look south on Mulberry Street at the tenement buildings with fire escapes projecting over the sidewalks:

Most of these buildings are of the late 19th-century New York tenement style known as railroad flats, five-story buildings on 25-foot by 90-foot lots. The rooms in each apartment are arranged in a straight line, like railroad cars, with no hallway on either side. The style was predominant in the densely populated lower Manhattan until 1901, when the city passed an ordinance requiring air shafts in the interior of buildings.

Mulberry Street has long been the heart of Little Italy, and at this point it's virtually the entire body. In 1932 an estimated 98% of the residents of the area were of Italian birth or heritage; since then the growth and expansion of Chinatown has encroached on the Italian neighborhood to such an extent that the merchants and community leaders of the Little Italy Restoration Association (LIRA) negotiated a truce in which the Chinese agreed to let Mulberry remain an all-Italian street.

Today Mulberry Street between Broome and Canal consists entirely of restaurants, cafes, bakeries, imported food shops, and souvenir stores. Some restaurants and cafes display high-tech Eurodesign; others seem dedicated to remaining precisely as their old customers remember them. How can you find the restaurant that's right for you? Perhaps by choosing the place that displays photos of the celebrity you like best: Sinatra, Cher, Dom DeLuise, Mayor Koch.

Former residents keep returning to Little Italy's venerable institutions. At the corner of Mulberry and Grand, **E. Rossi & Co.** (established 1902) is an antiquated little shop that sells housewares, espresso makers, embroidered religious postcards, and jocular Italian T-shirts. Down the street is **Ferrara's** (195 Grand St.), a nearly 100-year-old pastry shop that ships its creations—cannoli, peasant pie, Italian rum cake—all over the world.

❻ Umberto's Clam House (129 Mulberry St., tel. 212/431-7545), where mobster Joey Gallo munched his last scungili in 1973, occupies the northwest corner of Mulberry and Hester streets. Quite peaceable now, Umberto's specializes in fresh shellfish in a spicy tomato sauce. Yet another Little Italy institution, **Puglia** (189 Hester St., tel. 212/966–6006) is partly disguised as a restaurant where guests sit at long communal tables, sing along with house entertainers, and enjoy moderately priced Southern Italian specialties with quantities of homemade wine.

Around the corner on Baxter Street stands the **San Gennaro Church** (officially, Most Precious Blood Church, National Shrine of San Gennaro), which sponsors Little Italy's annual keynote event, the Feast of San Gennaro. When it happens each September, the streets become a bright and turbulent Italian kitchen.

Tour 12. Chinatown

In theory, Little Italy and Chinatown are divided by Canal Street, the bustling artery that links the Holland Tunnel (to New Jersey) and the Manhattan Bridge (to Brooklyn). However, in recent years Chinatown has gained an influx of immigrants from the People's Republic of China, Taiwan, and especially Hong Kong. Anticipating the return of the British colony to PRC domination in 1997, Hong Kong residents consider Chinatown real estate a safe repository for escape capital. Consequently, Chinatown has expanded beyond its traditional borders into Little Italy to the north and the formerly Jewish Lower East Side to the east.

Canal Street itself abounds with crowded markets bursting with mounds of fresh seafood and strangely shaped vegetables in extraterrestrial shades of green. Food shops proudly display their wares; if America's motto is "a chicken in every pot," then Chinatown's must be "a roast duck in every window."

The slightly less frantic **Kam Man** (200 Canal St.), a duplex supermarket, has fresh and canned imported groceries, herbs, and the sort of dinnerware and furniture familiar to patrons of Chinese restaurants. Choose from 100 kinds of noodles or such delicacies as dried starch and fresh chicken feet.

Mott Street is the principal business street of Chinatown. Narrow and twisting; crammed with souvenir shops and restaurants in funky, pagoda-style buildings; crowded with pedestrians at all hours of the day or night, Mott Street looks the way you expect Chinatown to look. Within the few dense blocks of Chinatown, hundreds of restaurants serve every imaginable type of Chinese cuisine, from simple fast-food noodles or dumplings to sumptuous Hunan, Szechuan, Cantonese, Mandarin, and Shanghai feasts. It may be hard to choose among them, but two things you can know for sure: (1) Every New Yorker thinks he or she knows the absolute flat-out best, and (2) at 8 PM on Saturday you'll have to wait in line to get into any one of them.

In the midst of the Mott Street hubbub stands the **Church of the Transfiguration** (Mott and Mosco Sts.). An imposing Georgian structure built in 1801 as the Zion Episcopal Church, it is now a Chinese Catholic church that delivers mass in Cantonese and Mandarin.

❼ Farther down Mott, the low-key **Chinatown Museum** explains the symbolism of flowers, chopsticks, and incense. A quiz game tests your knowledge of matters Chinese. *8 Mott St., tel. 212/964–1542. Admission: $1 adults, 50¢ children. Open daily 10:30 AM–midnight.*

Double back to Pell Street, a narrow lane of wall-to-wall restaurants whose neon signs stretch halfway across the thoroughfare. Turn onto **Doyers Street,** a twisty little byway whose storefronts house an extraordinary density of barber shops and the excellent **Viet-Nam Restaurant** *(see* Dining). Duck into Wing Fat, a new multilevel shopping mall that serpentines its way up, around, and out to Chatham Square.

❽ **Chatham Square** is the farthest thing from a square; it's more of a labyrinth, where 10 converging streets create pandemonium for autos and a nightmare for pedestrians. A Chinese arch honoring Chinese casualties in American wars stands on an island in the eye of the storm.

Two remnants of Chinatown's pre-Chinese past stand near Chatham Square. Walk down St. James Place to the **Shearith Israel** graveyard, the first Jewish cemetery in the United States. When consecrated in 1656, the area was considered outside the city. Walk a half-block farther, turn left on James Street, and you'll see **St. James Church,** a stately 1837 Greek Revival edifice where Al Smith (the former New York governor and a Democratic presidential candidate) served as altar boy.

Go back past Chatham Square and up the Bowery to **Confucius Plaza,** the open area monitored by a statue of Confucius and a high-rise apartment complex named for him. America's oldest drugstore, Olliffe's Apothecary, once occupied an adjacent building at 6 Bowery; now it's the Abacus Federal Savings Bank. At 18 Bowery, corner of Pell Street, stands one of Manhattan's oldest homes, a Federal and Georgian structure built in 1785 by the meat wholesaler Edward Mooney.

Time Out Take a break from Chinatown street life and things Chinese by ducking into the Canal Arcade, a passage linking the Bowery and Elizabeth Street. The **Malaysian Restaurant** is really a modest snack shop serving unusual Malay dishes (Singapore fried noodles, curried duck blood) and refreshing ices in flavors called Singapore, red bean, and lichee.

Head up the Bowery toward the grand arch and colonnade entrance to the Manhattan Bridge, and you'll soon return to Canal Street. The corner of Bowery and Canal was once the center of New York's diamond district. Many jewelry dealers have moved uptown (to 47th Street between Fifth and Sixth avenues), but a substantial number of jewelers still occupy shops on the Bowery and the north side of Canal. The selection is pretty good, and you shouldn't expect to pay the first price you are quoted.

Tour 13. Lower Manhattan

Numbers in the margin correspond with points of interest on the Lower Manhattan map.

Lower Manhattan is relatively small in area yet dense with attractions. The New Amsterdam colony was established here by the Dutch in

1625, and the first capital of the United States was located in the area. Wall Street is here, which means the New York and American stock exchanges plus innumerable banks and other financial institutions. Boats depart for Staten Island, the Statue of Liberty, and on ferry and excursion routes; the waterfront also inspired the South Street Seaport Museum project.

West Side
❶ Our West Side and East Side tours of lower Manhattan both begin outside the **Staten Island Ferry Terminal** at the southernmost tip of Manhattan. For subway riders, that's just outside the South Ferry station on the No. 1 line.

The **Staten Island Ferry** is still the best deal in town. The 20-to-30-minute ride across New York harbor provides great views of the Manhattan skyline, the Statue of Liberty, the Verrazano Narrows Bridge, and the Jersey coast, and it costs only 25¢ *round-trip.* A word of advice: While commuters love the ferry service's swift new low-slung craft, the boats ride low in the water and have no outside deck space. If one of the low-riders is next in line, you might be happier if you missed the boat and waited for one of the higher, more open old-timers.

To the west of South Ferry lies **Battery Park,** a verdant landfill loaded with monuments and sculpture at Manhattan's green toe. The **East Coast Memorial,** a statue of a fierce eagle, presides over eight granite slabs on which are inscribed the names of U.S. servicemen who died in World War II.

The steps of the East Coast Memorial afford a fine view of the main features of **New York Harbor:** From left to right, **Governor's Island,** a Coast Guard installation; hilly **Staten Island** in the distance; the **Statue of Liberty** on Liberty Island; **Ellis Island,** gateway to the New World for generations of immigrants; and the old railway terminal in **Liberty Park,** on the mainland in Jersey City, New Jersey.

Further along, you see a romantic **statue of Giovanni da Verrazano,** the Florentine merchant who piloted the ship that first sighted New York and its harbor in 1524. From here the Verrazano Narrows Bridge between Brooklyn and Staten

Island, the world's longest suspension bridge, is visible beyond Governor's Island.

❷ **Castle Clinton** may have gone through more changes than any other public building. Built in 1811 as a defense for New York Harbor, the circular brick fortress was constructed on an island 200 feet from shore. In 1824 it became Castle Garden, an entertainment and concert facility that reached its high point in 1850 when more than 6,000 people (the capacity of Radio City Music Hall) attended the U.S. debut of the "Swedish Nightingale," Jenny Lind. After landfill had connected it to the city, Castle Clinton became, in succession, an immigrant processing center, an aquarium, and now a restored fort, museum, and ticket office for the Statue of Liberty.

Castle Clinton is also to be the departure point for ferries to **Ellis Island,** set to open this year after a $140 million restoration, the largest-ever U.S. project of its kind (the fundraising drive was headed by Chrysler Corporation chairman Lee Iacocca). Now a national monument, Ellis Island was once a federal immigration facility that processed 17 million men, women, and children between 1892 and 1954—the ancestors of more than 40% of the Americans living today. *Tel. 212/883–1986. Admission prices and opening times not available at press time.*

❸ The popularity of the **Statue of Liberty** surged following its 100th birthday restoration in 1986. After arriving on Liberty Island, you can take an elevator 10 stories to the top of the pedestal. The strong of heart and limb can climb another 12 stories to the crown. Currently you may have to wait in line for up to three hours for the privilege. *Tel. 212/363–3200. Round-trip fare: $3.25 adults, $1.50 children. Daily departures on the hour 9–5; extended hours in summer.*

At the end of a broad mall outside the landward entrance to Castle Clinton stands the **Netherlands Memorial,** a quaint flagpole depicting the bead exchange that established Fort Amsterdam in 1626. Inscriptions describe the event in English and Dutch. Across State Street is the facade of the imposing **U.S. Customs House,** adorned by a double row of statuary. The lower

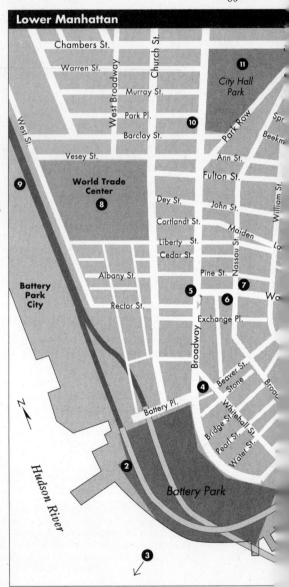

Lower Manhattan

Chambers St.

Warren St.

West Broadway

Church St.

City Hall
Park

❶❶

Park Row

Spr

Murray St.

Park Pl.

❶⓪

Barclay St.

Beekm

Vesey St.

Ann St.

Fulton St.

West St.

World Trade
Center

❽

Dey St.

John St.

William St.

Cortlandt St.

Maiden

❾

Liberty St.

Nassau St.

La

Cedar St.

Albany St.

Pine St.

❼

❺

❻

Wa

Rector St.

Exchange Pl.

Broadway

Battery
Park
City

Beaver St.

❹

Stone

Broa

Battery Pl.

Whitehall St.

Bridge St.

Pearl St.

Water St.

N

❷

Hudson River

Battery Park

❸

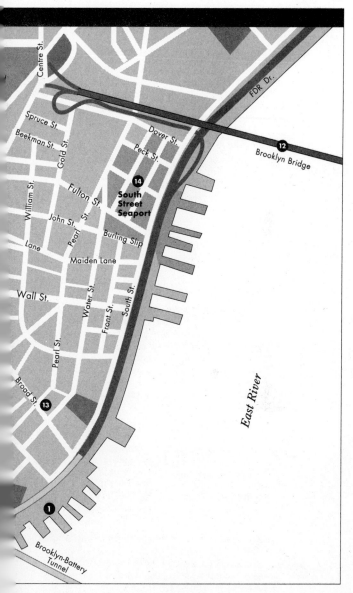

statues depict each of the continents; the upper row represents the major trading cities of the world (the woman to the left of the central shield stands for Lisbon).

❹ **Bowling Green** is an oval greensward that in 1733 became New York's first public park. On July 9, 1776, a few hours after citizens learned about the signing of the Declaration of Independence, rioters toppled a statue of King George III that had occupied the spot for years.

Broadway begins beside Bowling Green and continues north all the way to Albany. **25 Broadway** used to be headquarters of the Cunard steamship line. The ground floor is now one of the most spectacular post offices you'll ever see, a cathedral of gracious travel with sea gods and mermaids romping across the vaulted ceiling and walls, frescoes depicting great vessels of yore, and richly detailed wall maps of the seven seas. To the left of the vestibule, in a charming niche with an inviting fireplace, is a Philatelic Exhibition Center that displays and purveys commemorative stamps.

George Washington really did sleep at **39 Broadway,** not in the office building now occupying the site, but in the McComb Mansion, which functioned as the second presidential residence between February 23 and August 30, 1790, when it overlooked the Hudson River. The first presidential residence was at 3 Cherry Street, which would now be under the Brooklyn Bridge.

❺ Jet-black **Trinity Church** (Broadway and Wall St.) was New York's first Anglican Parish (1646). The present structure (1846) ranked as the city's tallest building for most of the last half of the 19th century. Alexander Hamilton is buried beneath a huge white pyramid in Trinity's south-side graveyard; Robert Fulton, the inventor of the steamboat, lies nearby. *Tours weekdays at 2; free 30- to 40-min concerts, Tues. 12:45.*

Arguably the most famous thoroughfare in the world, **Wall Street** was where stock traders used to conduct business along the sidewalks or at tables beneath a sheltering buttonwood tree. Wall ❻ Street's principal facility today is the **New York**

Stock Exchange, which has its august Corinthian main entrance around the corner on Broad Street. Enter at 20 Broad Street and, after what may be a lengthy wait, take an elevator to the third-floor visitors center. A self-guided tour, informative slide shows, video displays, and guides may help you interpret the chaos that seems to be transpiring down on the trading floor. *Tel. 212/656–5167. Admission free. Open weekdays 9:20–4. Tickets available at 12 Broad St., 9:15–3:45.*

In building only a two-story investment bank at the corner of Wall and Broad Streets, J. P. Morgan was thumbing his nose at Wall Street real estate values. Now **Morgan Guaranty Trust,** the building bears pockmarks near the fourth window on the Wall Street side, created when a bomb in a pushcart exploded in 1920.

A regal statue of George Washington stands at the spot where he was sworn in as the first U.S. president in 1789. The Federal Hall of that day was demolished when the capital moved to Philadelphia. The current **Federal Hall National Memorial** is a stately period structure containing exhibits on New York and Wall Street.

Walk through Federal Hall, past the gift shop, and turn right onto Pine Street. You soon reach a plaza around the 65-story **Chase Manhattan Bank Building.** The perimeter of Chase Plaza has become an impromptu flea market for merchandise and fast food, and the interior holds a striking Dubuffet sculpture, *Trees.*

Kitty-corner from the Chase Building, **Louise Nevelson Plaza** occupies the triangle formed by William Street, Liberty Street, and Maiden Lane. The plaza contains benches and four black welded-steel abstract Nevelson sculptures, three middle-size pieces, and one huge 70-footer. Sit in the plaza and contemplate the **Federal Reserve Bank** directly across the street. This is a bank that looks like a bank ought to look: gray, solid, imposing, absolutely impregnable—and it had better be, for its vaults reputedly contain a quarter of the world's gold reserves.

Across Maiden Lane from the Fed, take an escalator down to the **Whitney Museum of American**

Art, Downtown at Federal Plaza, a free museum that displays 20th-century American art.

8 Continue west on Maiden Lane to the **World Trade Center,** a 16-acre complex that contains New York's two tallest buildings, a hotel, a shopping center, a huge main plaza, and, somewhat incongruously, a farmers' market on Tuesday and Thursday in a parking area along Church Street. The Observation Deck is located on the 107th floor of 2 World Trade Center, yet the ride up takes only 58 seconds. The view is potentially 55 miles, but signs at the ticket window (Admission: $3.50 adults, $1.75 children) disclose how far you can see that day and whether the outdoor deck is open. You get the same view with a costly meal at **Windows on the World** atop 1 World Trade Center; prices are somewhat lower for breakfast or for drinks and "grazing" at the **Hors d'Oeuvrerie at Windows on the World** (tel. 212/938–1111). The TKTS booth (half-price Broadway and Off-Broadway shows) in the mezzanine of 2 World Trade Center opens earlier weekdays 11–5:30; Sat. 11–3:30) than the Times Square location and has shorter lines.

The rock and soil excavated for the World Trade Center begat **Battery Park City,** a hundred new acres of Manhattan reached by a pedestrian overpass above West Street on the western border of the center. Battery Park City is a complete neighborhood built from scratch. It has office buildings (including the offices of *The Wall Street Journal*), high-rise apartment houses, low-rise old-looking town houses, and a modest selection of shops. Gazing at the Hudson from the placid riverside promenade, you may find it difficult to believe that the New York Stock Exchange lies less than a half-mile away.

9 Battery Park City is also home to the **World Financial Center,** a mammoth granite-and-glass commercial complex designed by architect Cesar Pelli. Inside the four-tower structure is a melange of 30 upscale shops (including Ann Taylor, Barneys New York, Mark Cross, and Godiva Chocolatier), and a palatial public space called the Winter Garden. The room, adorned by a vaulted-glass roof, an immense stairway, and 16 palm trees (carefully transplanted from Borrigo

Springs, California), hosts an array of performances through the center's Arts and Events program.

Across Church Street from the World Trade Center stands **St. Paul's Chapel** (Broadway and Fulton St.), the second-oldest structure (1766) in Manhattan and the only surviving example of Colonial architecture. St. Paul's displays George Washington's pew and is open throughout the day for prayer, rest, and meditation.

⑩ Head north on Broadway to the so-called Cathedral of Commerce, the ornate **Woolworth Building** (Park Pl. and Broadway). Once the world's tallest building at 792 feet, this agglomeration of architectural styles still houses the Woolworth corporate offices. Gargoyles set into arches in the lobby ceiling represent old man Woolworth pinching his pennies and the architect Cass Gilbert contemplating a model of his creation.

Park Row, the street across City Hall Park from the Woolworth Building, was known as Newspaper Row from the mid-19th century to the early 20th century, when most of the city's 20 or so daily papers had offices there. Now the city is down to four dailies, and Park Row is an undistinguished commercial strip. In its day, triangular **City Hall Park** hosted hangings, riots, meetings, and demonstrations; much of the time now it accommodates brown-baggers and pigeon feeders.

⑪ **City Hall,** built between 1803 and 1811, is unexpectedly elegant, sedate, graceful, small-scale, and charming. Its exterior columns reflect the classical influence of Greece and Rome, and the handsome cast-iron cupola is crowned with the statue of lady Justice. The major interior feature is a sweeping marble double staircase. The wood-paneled City Council Chamber in the east wing is small and clubby; the Board of Estimate chamber to the west has Colonial paintings and seating in the church pew manner. Were it not for the metal detectors through which all visitors must pass, you'd think this was a county courthouse in rural Virginia rather than the epicenter of the nation's biggest metropolis.

12 Directly east of City Hall is the **Brooklyn Bridge,** New York's oldest and best known span. When built in 1883 it was the world's longest suspension bridge and, like so many others in turn, the tallest structure in the city. Now its graceful stone towers no longer seem so awesome. It hasn't been sold to a gullible out-of-towner for years.

Walking across Brooklyn Bridge is a peak New York experience. The distance is just over a mile, and thousands of commuters make the trip on foot whenever the weather allows. Located in the center of the span, the walkway passes beneath the towers and through the filigree. On the Brooklyn side the span bisects the expansive Watchtower complex operated by the Jehovah's Witnesses. Take the first exit to Brooklyn Heights, a charming neighborhood of brownstones, and head back toward the river to the Promenade for an exciting view of Lower Manhattan.

East Side Directly north of South Ferry stands the **Shrine of St. Elizabeth Ann Seton** (7–8 State St.). The red-brick Federal-style town house was built in 1783 as the home of the wealthy Watson family, and Mother Seton dwelled and gave birth to her fifth child in what is now the rectory. Mother Seton went on to found the Sisters of Charity, the first American order of nuns, and in 1975 became the first American-born saint. Masses are held daily.

East of the shrine, State Street becomes Water Street and passes **New York Plaza,** a complex of high-tech office towers linked by an underground concourse. Turn left on Broad Street **13** and you quickly reach **Fraunces Tavern,** a combination restaurant, bar, and museum that occupies a Colonial (brick exterior, cream-colored portico and balcony) tavern built in 1719 and restored in 1907. Best remembered as the site of George Washington's farewell address to his officers celebrating the British evacuation of New York in 1783, Fraunces Tavern contains two fully furnished period rooms and other displays of 18th- and 19th-century American history. *Broad and Pearl Sts., tel. 212/425–1778. Suggested contribution: $2.50 adults, $1 students,*

*seniors, and children, free Thurs. Restaurant
open weekdays. Museum open June–Sept.,
weekdays 10–4; Oct.–May, weekdays 10–4,
Sun. noon–5.*

Continuing up Broad Street and turning right
on South William Street, you enter an area of
curving streets (the routes of old New Amsterdam cowpaths) and low-rise houses that still
look much as they did in the 19th century.
Delmonico's, at the rounded corner of South
William and Beaver streets, opened in 1888. The
haute cuisine and one of America's first female
cashiers made it the place to go at the turn of the
century. Head east on William Street to **Hano-
ver Square,** a quiet tree-lined plaza that stood on
the waterfront when the East River reached
Pearl Street. The pirate Captain Kidd lived in
the neighborhood, and the brownstone **India
House** (1837) used to house the New York Cotton
Exchange.

⑭ Go one block east to Water Street and turn north
to the **South Street Seaport Museum,** part of an
11-block historic district that encompasses
shopping centers, historic ships, cruise boats, a
multimedia presentation, art galleries, and innumerable places to eat. In spirit linked more
closely to other Rouse Corporation waterfront
developments in Boston and Baltimore than to
the rest of Manhattan, the project still has a lot
of appeal.

Schermerhorn Row (2–18 Fulton St.), a series of
early 1800s Georgian and Federal-style warehouses, is the Seaport's architectural centerpiece. The ground floors are occupied by shops
and bars. The cobblestone street is closed to
traffic and, on Friday evening during summer,
young professionals from the Financial District
stand shoulder-to-shoulder at cocktail hour.
Markets have occupied the **Fulton Market
Building** site across the way since 1822. Now the
rebuilt structure contains shops, restaurants,
even a fish stall. The 15 restored buildings in
Museum Block, across Front Street, include
Bowne & Co., a reconstructed working 19th-
century print shop, and the Museum Shops
along twisting Cannon's Walk.

By day, the **Trans-Lux Seaport Theater** presents the multiscreen "Seaport Experience" hourly (Admission: $4.75 adults, $4 senior citizens, $3.25 children). At night it becomes an avant-garde cinema, showing foreign and American films.

Cross South Street to Pier 16 to view the historic ships: the second-largest sailing ship in existence, *Peking;* the full-rigged *Wavertree;* and the lightship *Ambrose. Admission to ships, galleries, walking tours, Maritime Crafts Center, films, and other Seaport events: $5 adults, $4 senior citizens, $3 students, $2 children. Open daily 10–5, longer hours in summer.*

Pier 16 is the departure point for the 90-minute **Seaport Harbor Line Cruise** (tel. 212/385–0791). The fare is $10 adults, $6 children. Notice how two large cargo containers used on modern-day freighters are transformed into a toy shop and a cafe.

Time Out Pier 17 is a massive dockside shopping mall. If you're hungry, skip the overpriced seafood joints and head for the fast-food stalls on the third-floor **Promenade Food Court.** Cuisine is nonchain eclectic: Third Avenue Deli, Pizza on the Pier, Wok & Roll, the Yorkville Packing House for meat, the Salad Bowl for veggies, Bergen's Beer & Wine Garden (10 brews on tap). What's really spectacular is the view of the East River, Brooklyn Bridge, and Brooklyn Heights from the well-spaced tables in a glass-wall atrium. Seating is on an outdoor deck when weather permits.

As your nose may already have surmised, the blocks along South Street north of the museum complex still house a working fish market. Although the city has tried to relocate the hundreds of fishmongers of the **Fulton Fish Market** in the South Bronx, the area remains a beehive. Get up early (or stay up late) if you want to see it: The action begins around midnight and ends by 8 AM.

Continue north to Peck Slip where, on the wall of a building on the north side of the street, you see a 90-foot trompe l'oeil mural by Richard

Haas showing how that view of the Brooklyn Bridge might have looked 100 years ago. Across the street stands an ornate co-op apartment that used to be **Meyer's Hotel,** where in 1883 Annie Oakley threw a wild rooftop party to celebrate the opening of the Brooklyn Bridge.

Off the Beaten Track

Public Spaces Public spaces go a long way toward making New York a more livable—and visitable—city. Public spaces are created when, in return for receiving a zoning variance, the builders of new office towers agree to design and maintain a portion of the interior space for public use. As such, public spaces perform roles formerly played by public parks and hotel lobbies: They provide clean, safe, physically attractive areas where you can sit, relax, read a newspaper, peruse your guidebook, and watch the world go by. You're welcome to stay as long as you like, and you don't have to spend a dime.

Many of the buildings that have public spaces have turned them into showplaces. And while each indoor park is unique, most of them have features in common. They provide places to sit, such as benches, ledges, and chairs with tables; they have greenery, from potted plants to towering trees; they have fountains or waterfalls to muffle the sounds of the city. Many have snack bars, working telephones, and, what can be very difficult to find elsewhere in Manhattan, clean public washrooms.

Buildings with public spaces identify themselves with a logo of a leafy tree over a checkered grid. Public spaces are usually open during the day, and many stay open late into the evening. The following public spaces are listed from Lower Manhattan up.

Continental Insurance Building (180 Maiden La. at Front St.). A modernist atrium just two blocks south of the South Street Seaport Museum. Benches surround copious foliage amid an ultramodern structure that appears to be made of Tinker Toys.

ChemCourt (272 Park Ave. between 47th and 48th Sts.). The Chemical Bank Building provides benches around plantings of exotic shrubs, all helpfully labeled in English and Latin. A glass roof lets the sunshine into the ground floor of the 50-story silver-gray tower.

Olympic Place (645 Fifth Ave., enter on 50th or 51st St.). A splendid space directly opposite St. Patrick's Cathedral and Rockefeller Center, on the ground floor of the brown-tinted Olympic Tower shop, office, and apartment complex. A wall of water drowns out exterior noise. Space includes a Japanese restaurant, a snack bar serving take-out sandwiches and pastries, washrooms, and phones.

Park Avenue Plaza (55 E. 52nd St. between Park and Madison Aves., enter on 52nd or 53rd St.). Conspicuous signs proclaim: "All seating available to public and no purchase of food or beverage required." Nonetheless, most of the tables are covered with tablecloths and table settings for an indoor cafe, and only a half-dozen tables and chairs at each end of the cafe are in fact available to the public.

875 Third Avenue (between 52nd and 53rd Sts.). Tables and chairs are on the mezzanine and basement floors. Basement seating is surrounded by an array of fast-food establishments: pizza, bagels, muffins, Chinese buffet, deli, salad bar. The basement also connects with the 53rd Street subway station (E, F lines).

The Market at Citicorp Center (Lexington Ave. and 53rd St.). The distinctive skyscraper whose roof slopes at a 45-degree angle has a thriving three-level atrium lined with restaurants, fast-food stores, and shops. Seating is at tables and chairs and along ledges. The center of the space frequently displays art exhibits or hosts free concerts and movies. Citicorp Center also encompasses the stunning Church of St. Peter's, a Lutheran institution that sold the land the building stands upon and now presents Off-Broadway plays and jazz concerts. Washrooms are on the lower level.

IBM Garden Plaza (56th St. and Madison Ave.). This most spectacular of public spaces has been carved out of the ground floors of the green-granite IBM building. Fully grown bamboo trees rise to the heavens, and seasonal flowers fill the air with fresh scents. The south wall and ceiling are all glass. Seating is available at comfortable chairs and marble tables and on benches beside the plantings. Sandwiches and pastries are sold at a charming round kiosk. The New York Botanical Garden operates a gift shop here, and the free **IBM Gallery of Science and Art** is located off the main lobby. Free concerts Wednesday at 12:30. The atrium connects to Trump Tower, which has phones and washrooms on its lower level.

499 Park Avenue (enter on 59th St.). This is one of the smaller public spaces, and the tinted black windows make it easy to miss. The atrium offers hard benches and a little calmness a block away from Bloomingdale's.

Other Attractions

The Cloisters. Perched atop a wooded hill near Manhattan's northernmost tip, the Cloisters houses part of the Metropolitan Museum of Art's medieval collection in a mock medieval monastery. Five cloisters connected by colonnaded walks transport you back 700 years. The view of the Hudson, the New Jersey Palisades (an undeveloped state park), and the towers of Manhattan far to the south enhance the experience. The No. 4 "Cloisters–Fort Tryon Park" bus provides a lengthy but scenic ride up there; catch it along Madison Avenue. You can also take the A subway to the 190th Street station. *Fort Tryon Park, tel. 212/923–3700. Suggested admission: $5 adults, $2.50 seniors and students, children free.*

General Theological Seminary (Ninth Ave. and 21st St.). This Episcopal institution opened in 1826 on a full city block contributed by Clement "'Twas the night before Christmas" Moore. A secluded Victorian quadrangle enclave of shady trees surrounded by proud ecclesiastical buildings, it is a pleasant refuge from workaday life. A 10-year restoration project is under way.

Roosevelt Island Aerial Tramway (Second Ave. and 60th St.). The high-wire ride to Roosevelt Island, a residential complex in the East River, looks like an oversize Fisher-Price toy. It is a slightly terrifying fun ride that gives you a great view of the city. The one-way fare is $1.

Playground at Sixth Avenue and Third Street.
Want to see where the NBA hoop stars of tomorrow learn their moves? Check out this patch of Greenwich Village asphalt where city-style basketball is played afternoon and evening in all but the very coldest weather.

Sniffen Court (36th St. between Lexington and Third Aves.). Here is an easy-to-miss cul-de-sac of 19th-century brick stables that were converted into town houses. Equal parts old London and New Orleans, Sniffen Court was for many years the home of the sculptor Malvina Hoffman.

East 90th Street Entrance to Central Park. At this open-air singles hangout for athletes, joggers congregate in the evening to chat, trade training tips, and occasionally run off together.

Paley Park (3 E. 53rd St.). Beside the Museum of Broadcasting, this was the first of New York's "pocket parks" inserted among the high-rise behemoths. A waterfall muffles street noise; a snack bar is open when weather permits.

McGraw-Hill Park (Sixth Ave. between 48th and 49th Sts.). The pocket park behind the McGraw-Hill Building has a stunning walk-through wall of water. Head west on 48th Street to Seventh Avenue, and you'll pass a half-block of stores that sell musical instruments.

Croquet and Lawn Bowling (Central Park, off Central Park West and 69th St.). Clad in spiffy white linen, the croquet players face off on this well-manicured patch of green almost every day of spring and summer.

Conservatory Pond (Central Park, off Fifth Ave. and 74th St.). Radio-controlled model armadas hold miniregattas every Saturday from April through November.

Duane Park (Duane and Hudson Sts.). Surrounded by striking 19th-century masonry buildings, this little triangle in the TriBeCa neighborhood is becoming one of the city's most fashionable addresses. Formerly the center of the dairy industry, horse-drawn egg wagons delivered here until 1954.

Staple Street (west of Hudson St. between Harrison and Duane Sts.). Named for the staple products unloaded here, this narrow alley was where ships in transit through New Amsterdam sold cargo they didn't want to pay duty on. An overhead passage connected sections of the former New York Hospital House of Relief.

Gansevoort Market (around Gansevoort and Greenwich Sts.). Otherwise undistinguished warehouse buildings each morning become the meat market for the city's retailers and restaurants. Racks of carcasses make a fascinating, though not necessarily a very pretty, sight. Action peaks on weekdays 5 AM–9 AM.

Ladies' Mile (Sixth Ave. between 18th and 22nd Sts.). Toward the end of the 19th century, the grand buildings on both sides of the street housed the city's finest department stores, including Simpson-Crawford, O'Neill's, Altman's, and Cammeyers. Trimmed with classical features but now fallen into disrepair, the vast Siegel-Cooper store occupied two-thirds of the block between Fifth and Sixth avenues.

Police Academy Museum (235 E. 20th St., tel. 212/477–9753). Here you can see an emergency procedures display, bizarre weapons, and the latest developments in law-enforcement technology. *235 E. 20th St., tel. 212/477–9753. Admission free. Open weekdays 9–3.*

3 Shopping

New York stores are as cosmopolitan and diverse as the city itself. The potential for high profits and world-class visibility motivates consumer-friendly competition at every level. Because merchandise has to attain a sufficiently high standard to please the world's most particular shoppers, costly boutiques and specialty shops abound. Because of the volume of competition in every area, close-out jobbers, off-price dealers, outlet shops, and other sources of discounts abound as well. Whatever you want, you can find it in New York. And if you look a little harder, you can find it selling for less.

In general, major department stores and other shops are open every day and keep late hours on Thursday. Many of the upper-crust shops along Upper Fifth Avenue and the Madison Mile close on Sunday. Stores in nightlife areas like SoHo and Columbus Avenue are usually open in the evenings. The bargain shops along Orchard Street on the Lower East Side are closed on Saturday.

Most of the department stores accept their own charge cards and American Express. Macy's, B. Altman, and Alexander's accept Visa and MasterCard. Most smaller stores accept major credit cards. Paying by personal check is sometimes permitted but seldom encouraged. Sales tax in New York City is 8¼%.

Shopping Districts

Upper Fifth Avenue. Fifth Avenue from 49th to 58th streets, and 57th Street between Sixth and Third avenues, contains many of the most famous stores in the world, among them Saks Fifth Avenue, Bergdorf Goodman, Henri Bendel, Bonwit Teller, Tiffany & Co., Cartier, and the exclusive shops in Trump Tower.

Herald Square. The area extending from Herald Square (Sixth Ave. and 34th St.) along 34th Street and up Fifth Avenue to 40th Street includes several major stores (Macy's, B. Altman, Lord & Taylor) and a host of lower-price clothing and accessory stores.

Madison Mile. The 20-block span along Madison Avenue between 59th and 79th streets consists of mainly low-rise brownstone buildings housing the exclusive boutiques of American and overseas designers.

SoHo. Along West Broadway between Houston ("How-ston") and Canal Streets you'll find art galleries, chic boutiques, avant-garde housewares shops, and shops that defy categorization.

Columbus Avenue. This shopping area between 66th and 86th streets features far-out European and down-home preppie fashions, some antiques and vintage stores, and outlets for adult toys.

Lower East Side. The intersection of Orchard and Delancey streets is the axis of bargains on women's and men's fashions, children's clothing, shoes, accessories, linens. Closed on Saturday; mobbed on Sunday.

Department Stores

Alexander's (Lexington Ave. and 58th St., tel. 212/593–0880). New York's least-expensive full-service department store may surprise you. The men's department features high quality attractive imports; women's sections reward sharp-eyed shoppers.

B. Altman & Co. (Fifth Ave. and 34th St., tel. 212/679–7800). A traditional, almost dowdy, establishment that caters to discriminating middle-income shoppers. It doesn't have the most fashionable collection of women's clothing, but menswear, furniture, and china are dependable buys.

Henri Bendel (10 W. 57th St., tel. 212/247–1100). A department store made up of many classy boutiques. Prices are not necessarily stratospheric, and window displays are always worth a close look.

Bergdorf Goodman (754 Fifth Ave. at 57th St., tel. 212/753–7300). A chic and very New York place to shop for women's designer clothes; you'll also find an underrated men's department.

Bloomingdale's (59th St. and Lexington Ave., tel. 212/705–2000). The quintessence of New York style—busy, noisy, crowded, and thoroughly up-to-date. Occupying the entire block of 59th and 60th streets between Lexington and Third avenues, "Bloomie's" adopts periodic themes (Hollywood, India, Japan, etc.) that permeate every display area. It's expensive but not outrageously so.

Bonwit Teller (4 E. 57th St., tel. 212/593–3333). Smaller since relocation in Trump Tower but still a stylish venue for high-fashion design.

Lord & Taylor (424 Fifth Ave. at 38th St., tel. 212/391–3344). Not flashy but a relatively uncrowded establishment that emphasizes well-made clothing by American designers.

Macy's (34th St. and Broadway, tel. 212/695–4440). The largest retail store in the United States occupies 10 stories (nine above ground, one below) and the entire block bounded by 34th and 35th streets, Seventh Avenue, and Broadway. Always comprehensive and competitive, Macy's has of late become quite fashionable as well.

Saks Fifth Avenue (611 Fifth Ave. at 50th St., tel. 212/753–4000). The flagship store of a nationwide chain has an outstanding selection of women's and men's designer outfits.

Flea Markets

Annex Antiques and Flea Market (Sixth Ave. and 25th St.; open weekends 9–5) consists mostly of antiques dealers selling furniture, vintage clothing, books, and jewelry. Admission is charged. The **I.S. 44 Flea Market** (Columbus Ave. and 77th St.; open Sun. 10–6) earns money for an after-school program by renting space to sellers of clothing, jewelry, books, and collectibles. There's a "Greenflea" farmers' market here, too. A lot at **335 Canal St.** becomes a beehive of treasures on weekends from March through December.

Farmers' Markets

Farmers from all over the area—from the tip of Long Island to Amish country in Pennsylvania —bring fresh produce, homemade breads and pastries, ciders, honey, cheese, butter, wine, even fresh fish to the **Union Square Greenmarket**

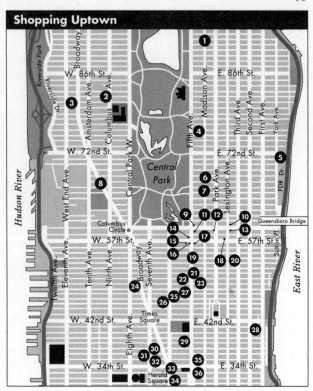

Shopping Uptown

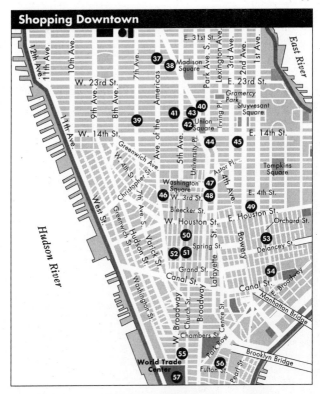

Shopping Downtown

Little Rickie, **49**
Lord & Taylor, **29**
Lubin Galleries, **38**
Macy's, **32**
Mark Cross, **21**
Ms., Miss, or Mrs., **31**

Museum of American Folk Art Gift Shop, **22**
Olden Camera, **34**
Pan Am Menswear, **54**
Paragon, **43**
Penny Whistle, **1, 2, 51**

Place des Antiquaires, **18**
Saks Fifth Avenue, **23**
Sotheby's, **5**
Stanrose, **30**
Strand Book Store, **44**
Syms, **55**

Tower Records, **8, 48**
22 Steps, **7**
Vieille Russie, **9**
Wholesale flower market, **37**
Ylang Ylang, **6, 16**
Zona, **50**

(Broadway and 17th St.; open Wed., Fri., Sat. year-round). Similar operations take place from about May through November in Greenwich Village (Gansevoort and Hudson Sts.; open Sat.); St. Mark's Church in the East Village (Second Ave. and 10th St.; open Tues.); West 57th Street and Ninth Avenue (Sat.); and along Church Street in front of the World Trade Center (Tues. and Thurs.). Greenmarkets generally operate from 8 AM until 6 PM but the earlier you arrive the better the pickings.

Specialty Shops

Antiques **ABC Antiques** (888 Broadway at 19th St., tel. 212/254–7171). Virtually a department store of antiques.
Place des Antiquaires (125 E. 57th St., tel. 212/758–2900). Two elegant subterranean levels of high-ticket antiques and art dealers.
Vieille Russie (781 Fifth Ave. at 59th St., tel. 212/752–1727). Fabulous pieces from Imperial Russia.

Auctions **Christie's** (502 Park Ave. at 59th St., tel. 212/-546–1000). Fine art at suitably fine prices.
Lubin Galleries (30 W. 26th St., tel. 212/924–3777). Reasonably priced furniture and antiques.
Sotheby's Arcade Auctions (1334 York Ave. at 72nd St., tel. 212/606–7409). The "budget" section of the exclusive auction gallery.

Books **Barnes & Noble Sale Annex** (105 Fifth Ave. at 18th St., tel. 212/807–0099). A two-story emporium of new books, used books, remainders, review copies, "hurt" books—everything at discount.
Gotham Book Mart (41 W. 47th St., tel. 212/719–4448). A browser's paradise of books on literature and the performing arts.
Strand Book Store (828 Broadway at 12th St., tel. 212/473–1452). A Greenwich Village institution with a vast selection of new and used books.

Cameras, **47th Street Photo.** (67 W. 47th St., 115 W. 45th
Computers, St., and 116 Nassau St., tel. 212/398–1410). A
Electronics chaotic sales floor, with no hand-holding but great deals on everything.
Olden Camera (1265 Broadway at 32nd St., tel. 212/725–1234). A creaky multilevel Herald

Square store where professional photographers shop.

Crafts **Folklorica** (89 Fifth Ave. at 17th St., tel. 212/255–2525). Ex–Peace Corps hands merchandise tasteful collectibles from Africa and other Third World locales.

Museum of American Folk Art Book and Gift Shop (62 W. 50th St., tel. 212/247–5611). The Rockefeller Center shop features a charming array of Americana.

Zona (97 Greene St., tel. 212/925–6750). This Soho emporium features handmade work from the Southwest.

Flowers and Plants The sidewalks are a jungle at the **Wholesale Flower District** along Sixth Avenue between 25th and 29th streets. They deal mostly with florists but happily sell retail.

Housewares **Conran's** (Citicorp Center, Third Ave. and 54th St., tel. 212/371–2225; 2248 Broadway at 81st St., tel. 212/873–9250; and 2 Astor Pl., tel. 212/505–1515). This is the store that furnishes those cunningly chic Manhattan apartments.

D. F. Sanders (386 West Broadway, tel. 212/925–9040; and 952 Madison Ave. at 75th St., tel. 212/879–6161). SoHo and Upper East Side locations for the slickest of Eurostyle high-tech housewares.

Jewelry Every store is a jewelry shop in the **Diamond District** (47th St. between Fifth and Sixth Aves.). Shop around—and be ready to haggle.

Fortunoff (681 Fifth Ave. at 54th St., tel. 212/758–6660). A discount jeweler in a flashy Fifth Avenue showroom.

Ylang-Ylang (806 Madison Ave. at 67th St., tel. 212/879–7028; 4 W. 57th St., tel. 212/247–3580; and Herald Center, 34th St. and Broadway, tel. 212/279–1428). Outrageous styles of costume jewelry at more or less affordable prices.

Leather and Luggage **Innovation Luggage** (10 E. 34th St., tel. 212/685–4611; 300 E. 42nd St., tel. 212/599–2998; and World Trade Center Concourse, tel. 212/432–1090). Large selection of styles at discount prices.

Mark Cross (645 Fifth Ave. at 51st St., tel. 212/421–3000). Fine traditional leather goods and solicitous service.

Fine & Klein (119 Orchard St., tel. 212/674–6720). One of Orchard Street's most illustrious discounters.

Menswear **Barneys** (106 Seventh Ave. at 17th St., tel. 212/929–9000). A Chelsea establishment that claims to be the world's largest men's store. Fine quality and substantial prices for traditional and high-fashion tailoring. Women's clothes, too.

Pan Am Menswear (50 Orchard St., tel. 212/925–7032). No gracious surroundings at this Lower East Side spot, but substantial discounts on brand names.

Syms (45 Park Pl., tel. 212/791–1199). Designer labels at bargain basement prices one block from the World Trade Center. Also women's clothing.

Records and **Bleecker Bob's Golden Oldies** (118 W. 3rd St.,
Tapes tel. 212/475–9677). A Greenwich Village spot with all the good old rock.

Colony Records (1619 Broadway at 49th St., tel. 212/265–2050). No discounts in this Theater District fixture, but a vast inventory.

Tower Records (692 Broadway at 4th St., tel. 212/505–1500; 1965 Broadway at 67th St., tel. 212/496–2500). A huge selection, with bargain prices, and a vibrant singles scene. Videotapes galore.

Sporting **Paragon** (867 Broadway near 18th St., tel.
Goods 212/255–8036). A three-level store near Union Square with reasonable prices on sporting goods, camping gear, running shoes, and sportswear.

Hudson's (97 Third Ave. at 13th St., tel. 212/473–0981). A huge operation with low prices on outdoor clothing and camping equipment.

Toys **F.A.O. Schwarz** (Fifth Ave. and 58th St., tel. 212/644–9400). A cathedral of childhood delights—with similarly lofty prices.

Little Rickie (49½ First Ave. at 3rd St., tel. 212/505–6467). Kid-size looniness in the wild and wacky East Village.

Penny Whistle (1283 Madison Ave. at 91st St., tel. 212/369–3868; 448 Columbus Ave. at 81st St., tel. 212/873–9090; 132 Spring St., tel. 212/925–2088). Upper East Side, Upper West Side, and SoHo locations for high-tone selection of European and American novelties.

Women's Clothing

Ms., Miss, or Mrs.—A Division of Ben Farber Inc. (462 Seventh Ave. at 35th St., tel. 212/736-0557). A Garment District establishment with new designer fashions at 40%–60% off.

Stanrose (141 W. 36th St. between Seventh Ave. and Broadway, tel. 212/736-3358). A no-frills Garment District outlet for up-to-date designer outfits at big discounts.

22 Steps (746 Madison Ave. at 65th St., tel. 212/288-2240). The name indicates how far you have to climb above Madison Mile for low prices on designer fashions.

4 Dining

Name any country, name any city or province in any country, and New York will probably have a *selection* of restaurants specializing in the cuisine of that area.

New York has more than 17,000 restaurants, from world-class temples of the culinary arts to humble cubbyholes serving pizza by the slice or hot dogs New York style, onions and sauerkraut optional. And while not even the most zealous New York food chauvinist would contend that every one of these places is fabulous, competitive pressures do effect a certain level of quality. No New York restaurant is likely to last long if its food doesn't taste good; few restaurants will survive if they don't serve reasonably large portions.

New York restaurants are expensive, yet savvy diners learn how to keep their costs within reason. Since most restaurants post menus in their front windows or lobbies, at least you will have a general idea of what you're getting into. But they don't post drink prices, and these can be high: $2.50 and up for a beer or a glass of wine; $3 and up for mixed drinks (some places charge *considerably* more). To run up your drink bill, many restaurants will ask you to wait in the bar until your table is ready. This occurs even when you have arrived on time and can see plenty of empty tables. While you may have to wait, you don't have to buy a drink.

One way to save money and still experience a top-echelon restaurant is to go there for lunch rather than dinner. It may also be easier to get lunch reservations on short notice.

Be sure to make a reservation when you intend to patronize a first-class restaurant. Be sure to make a reservation for *any* restaurant on a weekend, especially on Saturday night, when the only places that aren't filled up are the places you can live without. To limit no-show diners, many of the most popular restaurants insist that patrons reconfirm on the day of their reservation. Some restaurants will accept a reservation only if you supply a credit card number.

What follows is a selective list of New York restaurants serving a variety of cuisines in all price ranges in neighborhoods throughout Manhattan. As the list can by no means be comprehensive, some of the city's classic restaurants have not been included. In their place, however, you'll find some lesser-known eateries that are frequented by locals. The most highly recommended restaurants in each price category are indicated by a star ★.

Category	Cost*
Very Expensive	over $50
Expensive	$25–$50
Moderate	$15–$25
Inexpensive	under $15

per person without tax (8¼%), service, or drinks

The following credit card abbreviations are used: AE, American Express; CB, Carte Blanche; DC, Diners Club; MC, Mastercard; V, Visa.

American–Continental

Very Expensive ★ **Four Seasons.** Menus and decor shift with the seasons in this class act. The bright and spacious Pool Room has a marble pool, changing floral displays, paintings by Picasso, Miró, and Rauschenberg. It's the rosewood Grill Room, however, where movers and shakers rendezvous for Power Lunches. Both settings have wide open spaces, impeccable service—and very high prices. An imaginative and unpredictable menu puts an Oriental spin on traditional American and French cuisine. Duck au poivre and tuna steak are reliable choices. The Spa Cuisine menu appeals to weight-watchers; lower-priced pre- and post-theater menus (5–6:15 and 10–11:15) please wallet-watchers. *The Seagram Building, 99 E. 52nd St., tel. 212/754–9494. Jacket required. Reservations required, in advance for weekends. AE, CB, DC, MC, V. Closed Sun.*

Expensive **Gotham Bar and Grill.** A place with a name like Gotham better be huge, crowded, the quintessence of sophistication—and that's what this is. Owned by a former New York City commissioner, the Gotham Bar and Grill has a postmodern decor with tall columns, high ceilings decked with parachute shades, a pink-marble bar, and a striking pink-green-black color scheme. The menu is eclectic and surprising: Try duck roast carpaccio or roasted quail salad. *12 E. 12th St., tel. 212/620–4020. Dress: casual. Reservations advised. AE, CB, DC, MC, V. No lunch weekends.*

Odeon. A converted Art Deco cafeteria in the TriBeCa neighborhood south of SoHo and north of the Financial District, it's a lively place where everyone can feel at home. The menu mingles French brasserie-style dishes with purely American fare. Steak and *frites* or fettuccine in shrimp are always good choices. *145 West Broadway at Thomas St., tel. 212/233–0507. Dress: casual. Reservations advised. AE, DC, MC, V. No lunch Mon.–Fri.*

One If by Land, Two If by Sea. As the name implies, this restaurant has a Colonial past. It occupies a converted coach house once owned, like much of the rest of Greenwich Village, by Aaron Burr. Located on an obscure back street with no exterior sign, it can be hard to find. Inside, the elegant two-floor setting divides into a number of warm Colonial rooms. The menu features Continental specialties like steak, veal, and rack of lamb. *17 Barrow St. between W. 4th St. and Seventh Ave., tel. 212/228–0822. Dress: casual. Reservations required. AE, DC, MC, V.*

Moderate–Expensive   **Greene Street Restaurant.** A bustling SoHo cabaret where the quality of the food matches the high quality of the show. The vast bare-brick bilevel loft has dark romantic lighting and modern paintings all around. The menu features an eclectic selection of American, Italian, and French dishes—Dover sole and loin of lamb are recommended. Piano jazz accompanies nightly dinners; singers and comedians perform on Friday and Saturday nights. *101 Greene St. between Spring and Prince Sts., tel. 212/925–2415. Dress: casual. Reservations advised. AE, CB, DC, MC, V.*

Moderate   **B. Smith's.** Owned by former model Barbara Smith, this spacious and airy West Side eatery is frequented by black professionals and a pre-

Dining Uptown

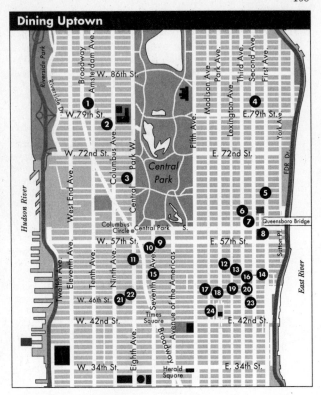

Alo Alo, **6**
Amsterdam's, **1**
Arizona 206, **7**
Auntie Yuan, **5**
Bangkok Cuisine, **11**
Blue Nile, **2**
B. Smith's, **22**
Bukhara, **19**

Café des Artistes, **3**
Carnegie Deli, **10**
Four Seasons, **12**
Grand Central Oyster Bar, **24**
Hatsuhana, **17, 18**
Le Bernardin, **15**
Lutèce, **16**
Nippon, **13**

Orso, **21**
Pig Heaven, **4**
Rosa Mexicana, **8**
Russian Tea Room, **9**
Smith & Wollensky, **20**
Sparks Steak House, **23**
Zarela, **14**

Dining Downtown

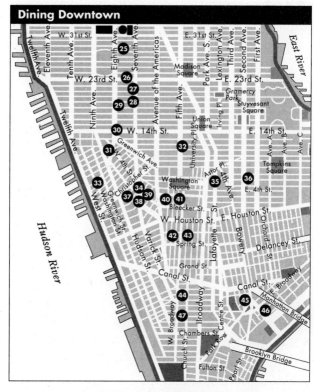

The Ballroom, **25**

Cafe de la
Gare, **33**

Cent'Anni, **39**

Claire, **28**

Cucina
Stagionale, **38**

El Quijote, **26**

Gotham Bar &
Grill, **32**

Grand Ticino, **41**

Greene Street
Restaurant, **43**

Indochine, **35**

Jane Street
Seafood Cafe, **31**

Mi Chinita, **29**

Minetta
Tavern, **40**

Mitali East, **36**

Mitali West, **37**

Montrachet, **44**

Nice
Restaurant, **46**

Odeon, **47**

Omen, **42**

One If by
Land, **34**

Quatorze, **30**

Thai Taste, **27**

Viet-Nam
Restaurant, **45**

theater crowd. Walls are painted in pale earth tones, tables are draped with white cloths, and artful arrangements of exotic flowers grace the room. The innovative menu ranges from "light plates" (such as grilled duck sausage over charcoal with coarse mustard and warm potato salad) to pasta (Maine lobster ravioli with a tarragon shellfish bisque) to hefty salads (warm roast chicken breast with wild mushrooms, wilted Napa cabbage, and toasted sesame dressing). Fresh seafood dishes—especially salmon and scampi—are also delightful. *771 Eighth Ave. at 47th St., tel. 212/247-2222. Dress: casual. Reservations accepted. AE, CB, DC, MC, V.*

Inexpensive   **Amsterdam's Bar & Rotisserie.** The name tells most of the story: It's basically a bar on the Upper West Side's Amsterdam Avenue where most of the food is prepared on an open rotisserie. Low prices for roasted poultry (chicken and duck are tops) and beef dishes accompanied by a vegetable and an ambitious house salad elicit standing-room crowds late into the night. Fish dishes are also good and homemade ketchup graces every table. *428 Amsterdam Ave. between 80th and 81st Sts., tel. 212/874-1377. Dress: casual. No reservations. AE, CB, DC, MC, V.*

Deli

Inexpensive   **Carnegie Deli.** This archetypal New York deli played a supporting role in Woody Allen's *Broadway Danny Rose.* Noisy and crowded, always in a frenzy, the Carnegie serves legendary corned beef hash and peppery pastrami, and merely great corned beef, chicken soup, and bagels. Special sandwiches may be named after the joker sitting at the next table. Portions are gargantuan—be prepared to walk away with a doggie bag. And don't let the brusque waiters get you down; they're part of the show. *854 Seventh Ave. at 55th St., tel. 212/757-2245. Dress: casual. No reservations. No credit cards.*

Chinese

Note: Chinese food is a staple of the New York diet. Most restaurants serve interchangeable

menus that combine dishes from various areas
of China and use a star or red lettering to indicate spicy dishes. With few exceptions the food
is good and truly inexpensive (less than $10 per
person). Chinese restaurants typically offer
low-priced lunch specials—soup, egg roll, main
dish, tea—for between $3.50 and $5. Restaurants listed here offer something more than the
typical neighborhood Chinese place. You can't
go wrong, either, with any busy restaurant in
Chinatown—the area bordered by Canal Street
on the north, and the Bowery on the east.

Expensive **Auntie Yuan.** The Upper East Side spot breaks
★ the mold of the standard Chinese restaurant. It
has high-gloss, all-black decor; pin lights focus-
ing on solitary flowers; and waiters ready and
eager to explain any of the dishes. Orange beef
and Peking duck are specialties; the tasting
menu is costly but full of strange flavors. *1191A
First Ave. at 64th St., tel. 212/744–4040. Dress:
casual. Reservations advised. AE, DC.*

Moderate **The Nice Restaurant.** This bright and shiny Chinatown mainstay can serve Hong Kong–style
dishes to over 400 people at a time on two floors.
By day (8 AM–4 PM), the Nice features *dim sum*,
bite-size dishes that you pick off circulating
trays. Favorite choices include dumplings (filled
with shrimp, pork, vegetables, or fish), pork
wontons, beef balls, and small coconut cakes.
The dinner menu contains photos of top specialties: minced squab in lettuce, deep-fried
prawns, roast suckling pig. *35 East Broadway,
tel. 212/406–9510. Dress: casual. Beer served;
bring your own wine. Reservations advised for
dinner. AE.*

Pig Heaven. This popular Upper East Side restaurant is gimmicky to the max. A cutout pig
greets you with the menu; wallboards are
painted a shocking pig pink; tea is served in
pigsnout mugs. Yet the food is serious. Pork
dominates the menu, with about 20 nightly specials available. Try Cantonese-style suckling
pig or minced pork sauteed with corn, peppers,
and pine nuts. Patience may be called for when
big crowds slow up the mostly non-Oriental
service staff. *1540 Second Ave. at 80th St., tel.
212/744–4333. Dress: casual. Reservations required. AE, DC.*

Cuban-Chinese

Inexpensive **Mi Chinita.** This frenetic Chelsea spot exempli-
fies a unique and ubiquitous type of New York
eatery: Cuban-Chinese restaurants. Operated
by ethnic Chinese refugees from Cuba, these
places do not allow the cuisines to mingle. Chinese dishes occupy one section of the menu,
Latin specialties another. Mi Chinita is an infor-
mal stainless steel diner with counter and table
seating. Latin specials (here, as at most Cuban-
Chinese places, the superior choice) involve permutations of shredded beef, pot roast, roast
pork, fried plantain, yellow rice, black beans,
and salad. Service is brisk, as lines frequently
trail out to the street. *176 Eighth Ave. at 19th
St., tel. 212/741–0240. Dress: casual. No reservations. Closed Sunday. No credit cards.*

Ethiopian

Inexpensive **Blue Nile.** Dining in this bright and spacious
basement on the Upper West Side near the
American Museum of Natural History is an experience. You sit on low, somewhat precarious
three-legged stools, and a mushroom-shaped
straw basket serves as your table. Folded sheets
of soft Ethiopian bread *(injera)* play a crucial
role. Dishes are served on it and you use other
sheets in lieu of silverware, to scoop up your
food. Most appetizers and entrees are easily
scoopable pastes and stews; everyone shares
everything. Try *afeza*, a spicy appetizer made
with lentils and onions, a hot chicken dish called
doro wot, and an Ethiopian rendition of steak
tartar. *103 W. 77th St. off Columbus Ave., tel.
212/580–3232. Dress: casual. No reservations.
AE.*

French

Very **Lutèce.** There isn't anyone who doesn't adore
Expensive Lutèce, a temple of classic French gastronomy
★ for over 25 years. The intimate and understated
midtown townhouse has seating around an en-
closed garden or in two more formal upstairs
chambers. The regular menu is varied and specials change daily; grilled trout and pheasant
are always fine choices. The impeccable service

is invariably attentive and helpful, to first-time
and hundredth-time diners alike. *249 E. 50th
St., tel. 212/752-2225. Jacket and tie required.
Reservations required 2 weeks or more in ad-
vance. AE, CB, DC, MC, V. No lunch Sat.-
Mon.; no dinner Sun.; closed in August.*

Expensive **Café des Artistes.** A romantic and extremely
popular Lincoln Center area institution. Murals
of nudes cavorting in a sylvan glade and spar-
kling mirrors transport you far from the
madding Manhattan crowd. Food is country
French with *confit* of duck and lamb with *flageo-
let* beans recommended specialties. The place
crowds up with West Side locals and out-of-
towners. *1 W. 67th St. at Central Park West, tel.
212/877-3500. Jacket required. Weekend reservations required 2 wks or more in advance;
weekday reservations required 2 to 3 days in advance. AE, CB, DC, MC, V.*

Montrachet. A neighborhood French restaurant
—the neighborhood is TriBeCa—that evokes
the flavor of backstreet Paris. Inside, the ambience is spare but attractive—wood tables with
white cloths, dusty-rose banquettes, carpeting
throughout—and the mood is chummy. The
menu favors fresh full-flavored Provençale-style
concoctions of seafood (black sea bass, lobster,
red snapper) and fowl (pigeon wrapped in cabbage, duck with ginger). *239 West Broadway
near White St., tel. 212/219-2777. Dress: casual. Reservations advised. AE. Closed Sun. and
1st week of July.*

★ **Quatorze.** A Parisian bistro on 14th Street, at
the border of Greenwich Village and Chelsea.
Quatorze ("14") is fancy but congenial, basically
a long and narrow neighborhood hangout with
plush banquettes, soft lighting, colorful French
posters. The menu is a brief and efficient card
highlighted by *choucroute*, roast duck, and lamb
medallions. The wine list is similarly brisk and
fairly priced, the service helpful and friendly.
*240 W. 14th St., tel. 212/206-7006. Dress: casu-
al. Reservations advised. AE. No lunch weekends.*

Moderate **Café de la Gare.** An intimate storefront on one of
Greenwich Village's quaintest streets. Both the
atmosphere—a handful of romantic tables

adorned with fresh flowers—and the menu are classic French. Cassoulet and seasonal preparations of veal, salmon, and game are specialties. Bring your own wine; call early for reservations. *143 Perry St., tel. 212/242–3553. Dress: casual. BYOB. Reservations required. CB, DC, MC, V. Closed Mon.*

Indian

Moderate–Expensive

★

Bukhara. This midtown spot features "frontier cuisine" from the northwest provinces bordering Pakistan. All entrees are either charcoal-grilled or roasted in *tandoors* (ancient clay ovens) and eaten without silverware (hot towels provided before and after). The menu provides vividly detailed descriptions of numerous chicken dishes, fish, prawns, beef. Hammered brass-and-copper trays and Bukhara rugs adorn rugged sand-colored walls. *148 E. 48th St., tel. 212/838–1811. Dress: casual. Reservations advised. AE, CB, DC, MC, V.*

Inexpensive

Mitali. The original Mitali is one of several Indian places on and around 6th Street between First and Second avenues in the East Village. Mitali West stands alone in the heart of Greenwich Village. Decor is somewhat elegant with red-jacketed waiters and walls faced with standard Indian prints. Menus feature Northern Indian specialties and bargain-price combination platters. Try Dopiaz curry or chicken tandoori. *Mitali East: 334 E. 6th St., tel. 212/533–2508; Mitali West: 296 Bleecker St. at Seventh Ave., tel. 212/989–1367. Dress: casual. Reservations accepted. AE, MC, V.*

Italian

Moderate–Expensive

Cent' Anni. Situated in a Greenwich Village storefront, this downtown favorite serves authentic Italian dishes to a discriminating native crowd. The interior, though spare, is tastefully decorated with wood furniture, fresh flowers, framed pencil drawings, and sketches of Italy. On the menu, you'll find such delicacies as rabbit with white wine, onions, carrots, and tomatoes; squid sauteed in oil, garlic, lemon, and spices; and linguine with tomato sauce, vodka, and red peppers. *50 Carmine St. at Bleecker St., tel.*

212/989–9494. Dress: casual. Reservations advised. AE.

Orso. A Theater District spot to meet before or after the show, Orso makes you feel you're in with the in crowd. It has an open steel-and-tile kitchen and walls adorned with celebrity photos. Theater folk congregate here for a brief menu highlighted by individual pizzas and pizza bread, and tangy pastas, and hearty entrees like striped bass with fennel and grilled quail in brandy sauce. The all-Italian wine list has a number of fine moderately priced selections. *322 W. 46th St., tel. 212/489–7212. Dress: casual. Reservations required up to 1 week in advance. MC, V.*

Moderate **Alo Alo.** People come to this sophisticated Upper East Side cafe for food and fun. Alo Alo is a glass-walled high-ceilinged chamber with papier-mâché statues perched atop lofty ledges. Ambient conversation is multilingual, mostly European, and the music is loud. Menu selections are fresh, bold, and light. Unusual pasta creations are best; the *risotto* special of the day is a good choice; fresh fish and veal selections will delight. *1030 Third Ave. at 61st St., tel. 212/838–4343. Dress: casual. Reservations advised. AE, CB, DC, MC, V.*

Grand Ticino. This casual 70-year-old Village favorite became an overnight success after inspiring the set for *Moonstruck.* (The movie was actually filmed elsewhere.) Located a few steps below street level, it is a simple and gracious setting for old standards like homemade *gnocchi al pesto* and *saltimbocca a la Romana. 228 Thompson St. between Bleecker and W. 3rd Sts.; tel. 212/777–5922. Dress: casual. Reservations accepted. AE, CB, DC, MC, V. Closed Sun.*

Minetta Tavern. Caricatures of local characters —artists, poets, playwrights, entertainers, bootleggers — and murals of Village landmarks adorn the walls of this hospitable old Greenwich Village hangout. The food is Italian, tasty, and moderately priced; risotto with shrimp, and breast of chicken Florentine are house specialties. But go there for the raffish flavor of Village life, as it was and as it remains. *113 MacDougal St., tel. 212/475–3850. Dress: casual. Reservations accepted. AE, CB, DC, MC, V.*

Inexpensive **Cucina Stagionale.** A truly good, inexpensive
★ Italian restaurant in the heart of Greenwich Village. It's a white-tablecloth storefront establishment with a selection of exotic pastas (spinach *penne* with seasonal vegetables, cold
lasagne with goat cheese) and meat specialties.
Main courses cost $6–$11 and you save even
more by bringing your wine. Not surprisingly, a
lot of people are on to this place, and lines can be
daunting; lunch is much more accessible. *275
Bleecker St. between Jones and Cornelia Sts.,
tel. 212/924–2707. Dress: casual. No reservations. BYOB. No credit cards.*

Japanese

Expensive **Hatsuhana.** The authenticity of Hatsuhana's
two bright and cheerful Midtown locations is
verified by conspicuous contingents of visiting
Japanese businessmen. They come for ultrafresh sushi and sashimi, which are best enjoyed
close up at the sushi bar. Other recommended
items include bite-size Japanese fried crabs,
ungreasy Japanese fried chicken, and any of the
grilled fish teriyaki. *17 E. 48th St., tel. 212/355–
3345; 237 Park Ave. at 46th St., tel. 212/661–
3400. Dress: casual. Reservations required for
dinner. AE, CB, DC, MC, V. No lunch weekends.*

Nippon. Recently relocated to its present address, this 25-year-old midtown establishment
serves traditional Japanese food in a traditional
Japanese garden setting. Specialties include
sauteed duck breast, tuna teriyaki, and soft-
shell crab. Try a little bit of a lot of things by or-
dering one of the "tasting menus." Or be very
daring and order something from the Special for
Connoisseur items like salted sea cucumber or
preserved herring roe. *155 E. 52nd St., tel. 212/
758–0226. Jacket required. Reservations accepted. No lunch Sat.; closed Sun. AE, CB, DC,
MC, V.*

Moderate **Omen.** Old brick, hardwood floors, timber ceilings, and Oriental lanterns give this SoHo ex-
store the relaxing ambience of a Japanese country inn. *Omen* is the name of an opening dish
almost everybody orders. It's a dark hot broth
served with half-cooked exotic vegetables, sesa-

me seeds, and noodles that you add to the soup.
Other favorites include a boned chicken dish
called *sansho*, scallops and blanched spinach,
and avocado with shrimp in miso sauce. *113
Thompson St. between Spring and Prince Sts.,
tel. 212/925–8923. Dress: casual. Reservations
advised. Closed Mon. AE, DC.*

Mexican

Expensive **Arizona 206.** The ambience of the American
Southwest is captured a block away from
Bloomingdale's: stark white plaster walls,
wood-burning fireplace, raw timber trimming,
and piped-in Willie Nelson records. Spicy New
Wave Mexican cuisine stresses chili peppers,
and the brief menu (by chef Marilyn
Frobuchino) offers nothing ordinary, only the
(likes of green chili paella for two; grilled salmon
steak with *poblano* corn pudding; and pistachio-
crusted tenderloin of rabbit with *mole poblano*
sauce. Desserts are just as unusual, and the
service staff is downright perky. *206 E. 60th St.,
tel. 212/838–0440. Dress: casual. Reservations
required. AE, CB, DC, MC, V.*

Zarela. Refined Mexican cuisine is served at this
Upper East Side spot. The menu features lightly seasoned *fajitas* (skirt steak), *salpicon* (red
snapper), and grilled raw tuna. Diners occupy
(heavy wooden chairs and brightly cushioned
benches which are positioned along a white
brick wall. Piñatas, crepe paper streamers, and
lively Mexican music add a festive touch. *953
Second Ave. at 51st St., tel. 212/644–6740.
Dress: casual. Reservations advised. AE, DC.*

Moderate **Rosa Mexicano.** This is a crowded midtown
★ hangout for young professionals. Serious dining
takes place amid subdued pink stucco walls and
lush horticulture. Two standard Mexican items
are exceptional here: chunky *guacamole* prepared at your table and margaritas blended with
pomegranate. Grilled versions of shell steak,
chicken, and snapper; pork *carnitas;* and
skinned breast of duck are other noncombusti-
ble house specialties. *1063 First Ave., tel. 212/
753–7407. Dress: casual. Reservations advised.
AE, CB, DC, MC, V.*

Russian

Expensive **Russian Tea Room.** Russian food is probably the last reason to eat here. Located beside Carnegie Hall, the Russian Tea Room is a major New York scene loaded with media people, their agents, and kindred would-be deal cutters. (Dustin Hoffman lunched here with his agent in *Tootsie.*) It's also filled with local commoners and out-of-towners, some of whom get exiled to the celebrityless second-floor—"Siberia." Best menu choices are hot or cold borscht, *karsky shashlik* (lamb with kidneys), and a selection of red and black caviars rolled into tender *blini* (pancakes). *150 W. 57th St., tel. 212/265–0947. Jacket required. Reservations advised. AE, CB, DC, MC, V.*

Seafood

Very Expensive ★ **Le Bernardin.** The New York branch of an illustrious Paris seafood establishment occupies the ground floor of the midtown Equitable Assurance Tower; the elegant corporate decor was reportedly inspired by the Equitable boardroom. The all-seafood menu teems with rare treasures. For starters, try black bass flecked with coriander or sea urchins baked in their shell. Go on to lobster in pasta or any of the fresh, artfully arranged fillets. *155 W. 51st St., tel. 212/489–1515. Jacket and tie required. Reservations required. AE, DC, MC, V. Closed Sun. and mid-Aug.–Labor Day.*

Moderate– Expensive **Grand Central Oyster Bar.** Down in the catacombs beneath Grand Central Terminal, the Oyster Bar has a reputation for serving ultrafresh seafood. The vast main room has a vaulted tile ceiling, and lots of noise and tumult. Solos may prefer to sit at the wide white counter. By contrast, the wood-paneled Saloon feels downright clubby. More than a dozen varieties of oysters may be on hand. Pan-roasted shellfish, a kind of stew, is a house specialty. Broiled fillets change with the daily catch. *Lower level Grand Central Terminal, 42nd St. and Vanderbilt Ave., tel. 212/490–6650. Dress: casual. Reservations advised. AE, CB, DC, MC, V. Closed Sat. and Sun.*

Moderate **Claire.** This lively Chelsea spot has a Key West
theme: hanging plants, trelliswork panels,
languid ceiling fans, skylights, a large airy
dining area. Whether or not it originated in the
Keys, all the seafood is fresh and tangy. Try
anything involving oysters or mussels, blackened
fish, Norwegian salmon. Naturally, the des-
sert menu includes Key lime pie. *156 Seventh
Ave. near 19th St., tel. 212/255–1955. Dress:
casual. Reservations advised. AE, DC, MC, V.*
Jane Street Seafood Cafe. Old wood, brick walls,
plank floors, bare wood tables, and low ceilings
import the cozy air of a New England pub to
Greenwich Village. The menu lists more than 50
seafood appetizers and entrees—we recommend mussels in broth and swordfish steak—all
accompanied by hot crusty bread and big bowls
of creamy cole slaw. Be prepared for a considerable wait at weekend dinner hour. *31 Eighth
Ave. at Jane St., tel. 212/243–9237. Dress: casual. No reservations. AE, DC, MC, V.*

Spanish

Moderate– **The Ballroom.** Located in Chelsea a few blocks
Expensive from Penn Station, this is the place to sample
tapas, Spanish appetizers that quickly accumu-
late into a full meal. Some like their tapas hot—
grilled eggplant, stuffed squid, baked fennel,
sauteed shiitake mushrooms, baby lamb chops.
Others prefer them cold—octopus in oil, bay
scallops, *chorizos* (sausage) with peppers,
chicken with tomato. The spacious, palmy setting focuses on a huge mural of local painters
and art dealers. A popular cabaret theater occupies a separate room. *253 W. 28th St., tel. 212/
244–3005. Dress: casual. Reservations advised.
No lunch Sat.–Mon.; closed Sun. and Mon.
AE, CB, DC, MC, V.*

Moderate **El Quijote.** A restaurant/bar on the ground floor
of the Hotel Chelsea, El Quijote has been a
haunt for generations of bohemians. The bois-
terous, popular neighborhood restaurant specializes in large portions and small prices. Lobster is the principal drawing card, with meaty
1½ pounders going for around $12.95. *Paella
valenciana* is another specialty, as are shrimp,
mussels, and oysters prepared in a variety of
Spanish sauces. *226 W. 23rd St., tel. 212/929–*

1855. Dress: casual. Reservations advised. Lunch and dinner daily. AE, CB, DC, MC, V.

Steaks

Expensive **Smith & Wollensky.** This midtown steak house opened only 12 years ago, but plank floors, bentwood chairs, and walls decked with classic sporting prints make it look like it's been here forever. Steak is the forte of this establishment, big blackened sirloins and filets mignon with a pepper sauce. Huge lobsters, veal chops, and terrific onion rings round out the menu. *201 E. 49th St., tel. 212/753-1530. Dress: casual. Reservations accepted. AE, CB, DC, MC, V. No lunch weekends.*

Sparks Steak House. Steaks and male camaraderie are the specialties of this midtown restaurant. The tender prime sirloin is the most popular selection. Filets are unusually juicy and flavorful; lobsters cruise the three- to five-pound range. Although most of the ex-athlete-size customers seem to go for beer or whiskey, Sparks boasts an award-winning wine list. *210 E. 46th St., tel. 212/687-4855. Jacket and tie required. Reservations required. AE, DC, MC, V. Closed Sun.*

Thai

Inexpensive **Bangkok Cuisine.** New York's oldest Thai restaurant operates out of an Orientalized storefront just north of the Theater District. Some of the spicy specialties include *tod mun pla* (deep-fried fish patties dipped in a sweet sauce), *pad thai* (an exciting noodle dish), and whole fish dinners. A small knife indicates superhot dishes—and here that warning means something. *885 Eighth Ave. at 53rd St., tel. 212/581-6370. Dress: casual. No reservations. No lunch Sun. AE, DC, MC, V.*

Thai Taste. No big scene here, just a cozy Chelsea neighborhood restaurant with good prices and friendly service. The small dark room encourages subdued conversation over traditional, exotically spiced Thai dishes. Some of the best are mussels in a sauce made with lime, and Thai-fried chicken. *208 W. 22nd St. at Seventh Ave., tel. 212/807-9872. Dress: casual. Reservations accepted. AE, MC, V.*

Vietnamese

Expensive **Indochine.** On the ground floor of landmark East Village town houses, the scene here mingles downtown artists with displaced French colonialists. The space is large and airy, decorated with palm leaves and tropical murals. The menu offers exotically spiced Vietnamese and Cambodian specialties. *Rouleau de printemps* (spring roll) is the standard appetizer; stuffed boneless chicken wings or steamed fish in coconut milk make excellent entrees. *430 Lafayette St. between Astor Pl. and E. 4th St., tel. 212/505–5111. Dress: casual. Reservations advised. AE, CB, DC, MC, V.*

Inexpensive **Viet-Nam Restaurant.** Down in a basement off one of Chinatown's most obscure streets, the Viet-Nam Restaurant is clean, friendly, and extremely inexpensive — most dishes go for less than $6. Many of the Vietnamese specialties involve exotic preparations of seafood and fowl. Try the shrimp pâté on sugar cane for an appetizer. Follow it with chicken in lemon grass or stewed curried duck. *11 Doyers St., tel. 212/693–0725. Dress: casual. No reservations. AE.*

5 Lodging

It's not just bad press: New York City hotel rates really have gone through the ceiling. Top hotels charge more than $200 per night for their humblest rooms, two or three times that amount for deluxe rooms and suites. Add combined state and city sales and hotel taxes of 13¼%, plus a $2 per room per night occupancy tax, and you're talking serious money.

Given the high going rate, New York also has many comparative bargains. Obtaining a bargain usually involves making a trade-off in the way of decor, amenities, service, and, primarily, location. Many acceptable lower-priced properties are located around the Theater District or a few blocks from the pricey Fifth–Madison–Park–Lexington axis. These accommodations are interesting, safe, and close to the fashionable neighborhoods.

On occasion New York can be a difficult place to find lodgings at any price. The average annual occupancy rate hovers around 80% and approaches 100% during the peak spring and fall seasons. Our listings include selected hotels in each price range, but it is far from being comprehensive. To receive a more exhaustive free list of hotels (no descriptions; just addresses, local and toll-free phone numbers, and rates), contact the **New York Convention and Visitors Bureau** (2 Columbus Circle, New York, NY 10019, tel. 212/397–8222). **Meegan Services** is a private company that locates and reserves rooms in all New York hotels; the service is free, and it operates 24 hours a day (tel. 718/476–5587 in New York; 800/472–6699 elsewhere).

Weekend Packages. When business travelers go home for the weekend, New York's hotel rates come down to earth. Virtually every New York hotel has a bargain weekend package that offers room rates approaching 50% off the regular weekday tariff. As further enticements, packages may include meals, cocktails, free parking, upgraded rooms or suites, theater tickets, guided tours, cruises, theme programs. Nearly all weekend packages apply to Friday and Saturday nights. Some apply to Thursday and/or Sunday nights as well. Some weekend deals require a two-day minimum stay.

To find out about weekend packages, contact a travel agent or request the free "New York City Tour Package Directory" from the **New York Convention and Visitors Bureau** (2 Columbus Circle, New York, NY 10019, tel. 212/397-8222). The Sunday *New York Times* Travel section usually has numerous ads for weekend packages.

The most highly recommended properties in each price category are indicated by a star ★. Unless otherwise indicated, all rooms have private baths and the hotel is open all year.

Category	Cost*
Very Expensive	over $200
Expensive	$150–$200
Moderate	$100–$150
Inexpensive	$75–$100
Budget	under $75

*double room; add 13¼% state and city tax, plus a $2 per night occupancy tax.

The following credit card abbreviations are used: AE, American Express; CB, Carte Blanche; DC, Diners Club; MC, MasterCard; V, Visa.

Very Expensive

Lower Manhattan **Vista International.** The only hotel in Lower Manhattan is part of the World Trade Center and, as such, shares its sleek glass-and-concrete exterior style. Close to Wall Street, the South Street Seaport, and the Statue of Liberty ferry but far from Midtown, the hotel tries a bit harder. It has a fully-equipped fitness center with an indoor pool and racquetball courts; it offers shuttle service to Midtown; the American Harvest restaurant is a showcase of American nouvelle cuisine. Weekend programs offer lower rates and an assortment of planned activities. Buses from all three airports stop outside the door. *3 World Trade Center, 10048, tel. 212/938-9100. 829 rooms. AE, CB, MC, V.*

Midtown **Grand Bay Hotel at Equitable Center.** The woe-begone Taft Hotel has been transformed into

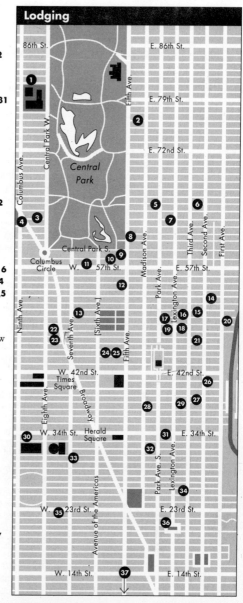

Lodging

one of the city's newest ultraluxury hotels. Paneled with Italian marble, the stunning lobby features 19th-century period furniture and bold floral displays. Unusually large rooms (averaging 450 square feet) come in eight different motifs, from Art Deco to country French; all have marble bathrooms equipped with tiny TVs. It's a short walk to the Theater District or Carnegie Hall. *152 W. 51st St., 10019, tel. 212/765–1900 or 800/237–0990. 178 rooms. AE, CB, DC, MC, V.*

Inter-Continental. The old Barclay Hotel is the local standard-bearer for the Inter-Continental hotel chain. The lobby is an opulent beehive of inviting leather furniture, a lovely Federal-style Tiffany skylight, and—one of New York's favorite rendezvous spots—a 14-foot-high brass birdcage. Rooms look elegantly traditional but function at state-of-the-art efficiency. Custom-designed cherrywood armoires conceal remote-control cable TVs and minibars. Guests can expedite the checkout process via their room TV. Several weekend packages are available. *111 E. 48th St., 10017, tel. 212/755–5900. 692 rooms. AE, CB, DC, MC, V.*

Peninsula of New York. New York's newest superluxury hotel inhabits the shell of the old (1905) Hotel Gotham; the decor harkens back to Paris of that era. Public areas express the turn-of-the-century Beaux Arts style, with lavish marble paneling and flooring, an 11-foot crystal chandelier, towering palms, and a sweeping marble staircase. Large guest rooms have the lush colors, carved French furniture, and marble trimming of the Art Nouveau era. *700 Fifth Ave. at 55th St., 10019, tel. 212/247–2200 or 800/2–MAXIMS. 250 rooms. AE, CB, DC, MC, V.*

Waldorf-Astoria. After a stem-to-stern renovation and restoration, the 47-story Art Deco legend where Guy Lombardo used to usher in the New Year looks as great as it ever did. The main lobby still has dark marble columns and the centerpiece bronze clock. Bas-reliefs, mosaics, and murals were all restored to their original 1931 grandeur. Rooms—nearly 100 fewer than before—are individually decorated in the Art Deco spirit. The flagship of the Hilton chain, its popular Peacock Alley bar is the home of Cole Porter's own piano. *301 Park Ave. at 50th St., 10022, tel. 212/355–3000. 1,692 rooms. AE, CB, DC, MC, V.*

Midtown– **The Pierre.** This fashionable 40-story Fifth Ave-
Central Park nue tower, managed by the esteemed Four
★ Seasons group, is far from being flashy. Public areas suggest the subdued entrance to a French château. High tea in the Rotunda is a truly European experience. Rooms radiate a quiet dignity with Chippendale furniture, chinoiserie, and, on the north, west, and south sides, stunning views of Central Park. Extra-care amenities include attended elevators, twice-daily maid service, 24-hour room service, in-room safes, and packing or unpacking service on request. *Fifth Ave. at 61st St., 10021, tel. 212/838–8000. 205 rooms. AE, CB, DC, MC, V.*

The Plaza. Even if you've never set foot in New York, you're probably familiar with the Plaza, which has appeared in more than 28 movies from *By Right of Purchase* (1919) to *Crocodile Dundee* (1986). Located adjacent to the southeast corner of Central Park, the venerable hotel, built in 1907, looks like a French château and has decor (crystal chandeliers, French Provincial furniture) to match. The new owner, Donald Trump, won't make radical changes; he can't alter the exterior because it's both a New York City and a national landmark. And he's promised not to alter the interior radically. *59th St. at Central Park South, 10019, tel. 212/759–3000 or 800/228–3000. 807 rooms. AE, CB, DC, MC, V.*

Upper **Mayfair Regent.** A dignified European-style ho-
East Side tel popular with corporate biggies and celebrities who prefer not to be recognized. The hushed lobby seems more like that of an apartment building—which this was until 1978 (some apartments still exist). The centerpiece lobby lounge is a refined setting for breakfast, light lunches, afternoon tea and cocktails; dinner is served in Le Cirque, a distinguished French restaurant. Rooms have Early American decor augmented with butler's pantries, humidifiers, and at least two phones. Attendant-operated elevators run at all times. *610 Park Ave. at 65th St., 10021, tel. 212/288–0800. 200 rooms. AE, CB, MC, V.*

Expensive

Midtown
★

Algonquin. A venerable (opened 1902) but up-to-date and extremely well-maintained hotel with a long literary history. The illustrious Round Table convened here in the 1920s and *New Yorker* staff and contributors frequent its bars and restaurants today. The oak-paneled lobby projects the gracious antiquated atmosphere of an English club. Rooms are quiet and cozy, furnished in Early American style with inviting brass beds. Its lobby lounge and Rose Room get lively after curtains fall in the nearby Theater District. The Oak Room is a sophisticated cabaret. *59 W. 44th St., 10036, tel. 212/840–6800 or 800/548–0345. 165 rooms. AE, CB, DC, MC, V.*

Halloran House. This is a hitherto unexceptional midtown hotel that's committed to improvement. A year-long project has completely renovated all guest rooms, lounge areas, and restaurants. Three nonsmoking floors and a top-12-floor executive club have been added. There are good views of the East River on east side floors. For the location—kitty-corner to the Waldorf—you can't beat the good deal. *525 Lexington Ave. between 48th and 49th Sts., 10017, tel. 212/755–4000 or 800/223–0939. 652 rooms. AE, CB, MC, V.*

Midtown–Murray Hill

Morgans. It's so unhotellike that no sign betrays its presence and nothing in the ground-floor reception area indicates that this is anything but an exclusive apartment house. The name comes from the Pierpont Morgan Library on the next block. Operated by the folks who created Studio 54 and the Palladium disco, Morgans appeals to upper-rung businesspeople and show folk. (Cher stayed for a month.) Smallish rooms have high-tech trappings in black, white, and various shades of gray; all rooms have down comforters, VCRs, and cassette decks. The brightest rooms and best views are on the east side. At press time, Morgans did not have a liquor license. *237 Madison Ave. at 37th St., 10016, tel. 212/686–0300 or 800/334–3408. 154 rooms. AE, CB, DC, MC, V.*

Midtown–Upper East Side **Manhattan East Suite Hotels.** This is a chain of nine well-appointed Midtown and Upper East Side properties that offer suites for what other hotels charge for rooms. Configurations vary; studio suites have oversize sleeping rooms and dining or sitting areas; junior suites have living rooms and separate sleeping areas; one-, two-, and three-bedroom suites have separate bedrooms. All accommodations have kitchens equipped with glassware, dishes, silverware, and cooking utensils. It's a great deal for families. *Beekman Tower, 3 Mitchell Pl. (near the U.N.), 10017, 160 rooms; Dumont Plaza, 150 E. 34th St., 10016, 251 rooms; Eastgate Tower, 222 E. 39th St., 10016, 191 rooms; Lyden Gardens, 215 E. 64th St., 10021, 133 rooms; Lyden House, 320 E. 53rd St., 10022, 81 rooms; Plaza 50, 155 E. 50th St., 10022, 206 rooms; Shelburne Murray Hill, 303 Lexington Ave. at 37th St., 10016, 248 rooms; Southgate Tower, 371 Seventh Ave. at 31st St., 10001, 522 rooms; Surrey Hotel, 20 E. 76th St., 10021, 117 rooms. Tel. 800/637–8483. AE, DC, MC, V.*

Upper East Side **Barbizon Hotel.** For 50 years it was a residence for "young ladies of good breeding" (Grace Kelly and Liza Minnelli among many others); now it's a privately run hotel. The atmosphere is elegant but livable. The lobby resembles a cloister with stone pillars rising to a trompe l'oeil mural of garden trellises. Rooms are a bit small but made bright with soft Barbizon school of art colors, country French furnishings, and original posters. The Barbizon Café has a menu that includes filet of Norwegian salmon, sauteed breast of chicken, and fresh spinach pasta with bay scallops. *140 E. 63rd St., 10021, tel. 212/838–5700. 368 rooms. AE, CB, DC, MC, V.*

Moderate

Lower Midtown **Gramercy Park.** Location and value are the two main assets. It's directly opposite charming Gramercy Park, a London-style square that stays charming by means of a wrought-iron fence and locked gates, which only residents can open. The hotel itself isn't nearly as special, but it's a clean, unpretentious, and moderately priced place popular with foreign visitors. Good bargains on one-bedroom suites. Ask for south

(Gramercy Park) views. *2 Lexington Ave. at 21st St., 10010, tel. 212/475-4320 or 800/221-4083. 500 rooms. AE, CB, DC, MC, V.*

Midtown

Salisbury. An attractive and well-maintained hotel priced at the lower end of Moderate on 57th Street opposite Carnegie Hall. Rooms aren't fancy but they're reasonably large and furnished in Early American decor with original paintings. All rooms contain safes and 95% have a refrigerator and pantry. *123 W. 57th St., 10019, tel. 212/246-1300 or 800/223-0680. 320 rooms. AE, CB, DC, MC, V.*

Midtown–Central Park ★

Wyndham. Everybody's New York secret, Wyndham is a cozy, friendly, impeccably maintained hotel at the low end of the Moderate range, just a half-block from The Plaza. It's popular with show-biz types from the other coast making lengthy sojourns. They appreciate homey effects like buzz-in front doors, attended elevators, personal but not cloying special treatment. Rooms are individually decorated with bright floral wallpaper and comfy furniture. Great deals are available on large suites with refrigerators and pantries. *42 W. 58th St., 10019, tel. 212/753-3500. 200 rooms. AE, CB, DC, MC, V.*

Midtown–United Nations

Chatwal Inn at the UN. This 1920s Tudor Gothic apartment complex, formerly the Hotel Tudor, stands at the east end of 42nd Street, a few blocks from the United Nations. A surprisingly good bargain for the location, the hotel is usually filled with foreign guests. Rooms are bright and recently refurbished. Public areas are a bit run-down but new owners are undertaking major renovations. *304 E. 42nd St., 10017, tel. 212/986-8800 or 800/221-1253. 500 rooms. AE, DC, MC, V.*

West Side–Lincoln Center

Empire Hotel. Those who recall the faded old Empire will hardly recognize it now. The place has been transformed. The marble pillars and high ceilings in the lobby are brightened up and completely restored. The rooms are repainted with restful pastels and redecorated with dignified cherry mahogany furniture. But even though it's added a corporate program to entice a new clientele of business travelers, the relatively low rates and Lincoln Center location still attract mainly musicians, music lovers, and tin-eared bargain-hunters. *44 W. 63rd St. at Broadway, 10023, tel. 212/265–7400. 500 rooms. AE, CB, DC, MC, V.*

Inexpensive

Chelsea **Hotel Chelsea.** This hotel can be an experience —although perhaps not everyone's favorite experience. An imposing red-brick building with New Orleans–style wrought-iron balconies, the 1882 structure was the first hotel proclaimed a national landmark. Generations of creative people have stayed or lived here, from Mark Twain, Thomas Wolfe, Dylan Thomas, and Arthur Miller to Lenny Bruce, Jane Fonda, William Burroughs, and Sid Vicious. The facade was recently spruced up, and wild contemporary art brightens the tiny lobby. Rooms, though large, have Fleabag Modern decor, and you may feel uncomfortable sharing an elevator with some of the other guests. Only half the rooms are air-conditioned; they cost more, but they are the only way to go in summer. *222 W. 23rd St., 10011, tel. 212/243–3700. 400 rooms. AE, MC, V.*

Midtown **Hotel Iroquois.** This bargain property near the
★ Theater District and Grand Central Terminal is turning into a small gem. The smallish lobby is already colored a welcoming shade of pink. Renovated guest rooms have an Early American decor; less expensive unrenovated rooms are decorated in Early Stopgap. The enthusiastic and helpful staff speak 14 languages. Jan Wallman's, a popular cabaret, is on the ground floor. Many suites are available for less than $100. *49 W. 44th St., 10036, tel. 212/840–3080 or 800/332–7220. 125 rooms. AE, CB, DC, MC, V.*

Midtown– **Chatwal Inn.** The former Hotel President has
Theater been transformed inside and out. The old facade
District has been covered with stone and augmented with a brass canopy. The all new lobby is paneled with marble, illuminated by a skylight, and foliated by lofty palm trees. The rooms, though a bit small, have pleasantly pink wallpaper and sleek new Art Deco furnishings. This flagship of the growing Chatwal chain is popular with groups of overseas visitors. *234 W. 48th St.,*

10036, tel. 212/246–8800 or 800/262–4665. 400 rooms. AE, CB, DC, MC, V.

Hotel Edison. This is a huge and bustling establishment a half-block from Broadway. Popular with entertainers and theater lovers from around the world, its busy Art Deco lobby offers comfy chairs perfectly positioned for people-watching. The Cafe Edison, or the Polish Tea Room, serves hearty Eastern European dishes (kasha, cabbage soup) to deal-making show-biz types and a regular clique of magicians. Request a bright and pleasantly furnished room in one of the renovated sections. *228 W. 47th St., 10036, tel. 212/840–5000 or 800/637–7070. 1,000 rooms. AE, CB, DC, MC, V.*

Upper West Side **Excelsior.** A budget property a block from Central Park, opposite the American Museum of Natural History, at the northern end of the Columbus Avenue commercial strip. Heavily booked with Europeans and people with museum business, the newly decorated guest rooms offer no-frills-but-nice decor. It cherishes a reputation as a decent, family-oriented establishment that won't book conventioneers and other raucous types. *45 W. 81st St., 10024, tel. 212/362–9200. 300 rooms. AE, MC, V.*

Budget

Hotels in this category have at least some rooms for $50 a night or less. These may be single rooms or rooms with shared baths.

Midtown **Grand Union.** This is a bargain in a reasonably safe area, literally in the shadow of the Empire State Building. Rooms have been newly remodeled with decent motel-style furniture, and are popular with European travelers. All rooms have window air conditioners and AM/FM alarm-clock/cable TV. A small lobby and the Grand Burger coffee shop comprise the public space. Rooms with shared baths (the baths are shared by two or three rooms) cost $50 per night single or double; rooms with private bath begin at $60. *34 E. 32nd St., 10016, tel. 212/683–5890. 95 rooms. AE, MC, V.*

New Carlton Arms. Call this an adventure in lodging, where management has turned avant-garde artists loose on a lower-midtown quasiflophouse. Rooms in "Artbreak Hotel" may represent the inside of a submarine, the lost city of Atlantis, or a Hindu temple. Rooms are spartan —small, minimally furnished, no TV, no phone —and management admits they're not for everybody: "Guests who like us best are usually students, backpacking international tourists, artists, musicians, actors . . ." It's clean, secure, convenient, and cheap—singles with shared bath are $33, doubles are $44; private baths cost $6 more. Students (with ID) and foreign tourists (with passports) get about 20% off. *160 E. 25th St., 10010, tel. 212/679–0680. 54 rooms. MC, V.*

★ **Pickwick Arms Hotel.** This convenient East Side establishment charges $75 a night for standard renovated doubles but has older singles with shared baths for as little as $42. Rooms are comfortably furnished in white bamboo. The lobby has been recently redecorated and guests have access to a roof garden. The ground-floor Beekman Gourmet Deli sells sandwiches, soft drinks, beer, snacks, and other necessities of life. *230 E. 51st St., 10022, tel. 212/355–0300 or 800/PICKWIK. 400 rooms. AE, CB, DC, MC, V.*

YMCA

Three Manhattan Ys offer men and women unexpectedly convenient locations for low-price lodging plus exercise facilities, budget cafeterias, and plenty of opportunities to mingle with fellow guests. No-frills rooms are usually in the $30–$40 range for singles or doubles; most have shared baths. Ys are heavily booked in peak seasons and often require deposits or advance payment.

The 561-room **West Side Y** (5 W. 63rd St., 10023, tel. 212/787–4400) is a half-block from Central Park and around the corner from Lincoln Center. *MC, V.* The 438-room **Vanderbilt YMCA** (224 E. 47th St., 10017, tel. 212/755–2410) is on the East Side, not far from the United Nations Headquarters. *MC, V.* The huge 1,490-room **Sloane House YMCA** (356 W. 34th St., 10001, tel. 212/760–5860) is near Penn Station and just a few blocks south of the Theater District. *No credit cards.*

Bed-and-Breakfast

Hundreds of rooms are available on a bed-and-breakfast basis in Manhattan and the most proximate areas of the outer boroughs, principally Brooklyn. B&Bs almost always cost well below $100 a night; some singles are available for under $50.

New York B&Bs, however, are not the quaint old mansions you find in other localities. They fall into two categories: (1) *Hosted apartments*, a bedroom in an apartment where the host is present; (2) *unhosted apartments*, entire apartments that are temporarily vacant. The unhosted option is scarcer and somewhat more expensive.

Along with saving money, B&Bs permit you to mingle with New Yorkers and stay in "real" neighborhoods rather than tourist ghettos. The disadvantages are that accommodations, amenities, service, and privacy fall far short of what you get in hotels. Sometimes you really do get breakfast and sometimes you don't. And you usually can't pay by credit card.

Here are reservation agencies that book B&B accommodations in and near Manhattan. There is no fee for the service, but they advise you to make reservations as far in advance as possible. It's a good idea to find out something about the city before you contact them, and then to request accommodations in a neighborhood that you prefer.

Bed and Breakfast Network of New York (134 W. 32nd St., Suite 602, New York, NY 10001, tel. 212/645–8134).
City Lights Bed and Breakfast, Ltd. (Box 20355, Cherokee Station, New York, NY 10028, tel. 212/737–7049).
New World Bed and Breakfast (150 Fifth Ave., Suite 711, New York, NY 10011, tel. 212/675–5600 or 800/443–3800).
Urban Ventures (306 W. 38th St., New York, NY 10018, tel. 212/594–5650).

6 The Arts and Nightlife

The Arts

Full listings of weekly entertainment and cultural events appear in *New York* magazine; they include capsule summaries of Broadway, Off-Broadway, and Off-Off-Broadway shows and concerts, performance times, and ticket prices. The Arts & Leisure section of the Sunday *New York Times* lists and describes events but provides no service information. The Theater Directory in the daily *New York Times* advertises ticket information for Broadway and Off-Broadway shows. Listings of arts events appear weekly in *The New Yorker* and *Village Voice*.

Theater

New York theater is the benchmark for quality and variety. At the height of the season, theatergoers might see anything from full-scale star-studded Broadway musicals to experimental happenings at nearly 40 Broadway theaters, three dozen Off-Broadway theaters, and 200 Off-Off-Broadway houses. The differences among the three tiers of New York theater can be seen in the level of professionalism of the performers, the location and opulence of the auditorium, and the price of the ticket.

Broadway theaters are located in the Theater District, most of which lies between Broadway and Eighth Avenue, from 43rd to 52nd streets. Some of these theaters are small gems, comfortable and luxurious yet intimate enough to make the audience feel part of the show. The newer, larger theaters are no less luxurious. All performers work under an Actors Equity contract that guarantees them a basic minimum salary. Ticket prices range from $22.50 to $55, depending on the show, the time of performance, and the location of the seat. Generally, plays are less expensive than musicals; and matinees (Wednesday, Saturday, and sometimes Sunday) and weeknight performances cost less than shows on Friday and Saturday nights. Most Broadway theaters are "dark" (closed) on Monday, although some are dark on other days.

Off-Broadway theater has professional performers but generally less elaborate productions. The theaters are located all over town. Many can be found along a strip of 42nd Street between Ninth and Tenth avenues; others are in Greenwich Village, the Upper East Side, Chelsea, Harlem, and Brooklyn. Ticket prices range from $10 to $30, with most falling into the $20–$25 range.

Off-Off-Broadway theater is alternative theater. Performers and production staff may be professionals, but they get little or no salary. Although you won't find lavish sets and plush seating, plays can be highly professional—with performances of everything from Shakespeare to the work of a soon-to-be-discovered genius. Off-Off-Broadway houses are located in all kinds of spaces—lofts, church basements, converted storefronts—all over town. Tickets rarely exceed $10, and you can phone ahead for reservations. *New York* magazine contains the best information on Off-Off-Broadway shows.

It's easy to buy tickets for Broadway and Off-Broadway shows; you can do it even before you reach New York. All Broadway show tickets are available by phone from either **Tele-Charge** (tel. 212/239–6200) or **Teletron** (tel. 212/246–0102). You pay the price of the tickets plus a surcharge to a major credit card and pick them up at the box office before the show. Both of these services operate 24 hours a day, seven days a week. Similar arrangements are available for Off-Broadway through **Hit-Tix** (tel. 212/564–8038), **Ticketmaster** (tel. 212/307–7171), or individual theaters.

In New York, you can buy Broadway tickets at the box offices, which are open most of the day and all evening. Tickets for many Off-Broadway shows are available at **Ticket Central** (416 W. 42nd St., tel. 212/279–4200). Tickets for the hottest shows in town—of late *The Phantom of the Opera*, and *Les Misérables*—may be available only through ticket brokers. Brokers in New York can sell the ticket for full price plus a *legal* surcharge of $2.50 per ticket; consequently, many operate out of New Jersey where such limits don't apply. Look them up in the Manhattan

Yellow Pages under "Ticket Sales—Entertainment & Sports."

For discounts of nearly 50% on Broadway and Off-Broadway shows, you can try your luck at **TKTS** (tel. 212/354–5800). This nonprofit service sells day-of-performance tickets for half the regular price, plus a $1.50 per ticket service charge. Supply is erratic. Sometimes it seems that every show in town appears on the display board just outside the ticket window. At other times only long-running hits and little-known sleepers are available.

The main TKTS booth is located in the Theater District on Duffy Square, a triangle formed by Broadway, Seventh Avenue, and 47th Street. It's open from 3 to 8 PM daily for evening performances, 10 to 2 for Wednesday and Saturday matinees, and noon to 8 for Sunday matinee and evening performances. A TKTS booth at 2 World Trade Center opens earlier in the day and generally has shorter lines. Its hours are weekdays from 11 to 5:30, Saturday from 11:30 to 3:30. Matinee and Sunday tickets are sold the day before the performance; Off-Broadway tickets are sold 11 AM to 1 PM for evening performances only. Another TKTS booth in front of Borough Hall in Brooklyn (tel. 718/625–5015) operates Tuesday–Friday 11–5:30 and Saturday 11–3:30 for evening performances only. Matinee and Sunday tickets are available the day before the performance; Off-Broadway tickets are sold only until 1 PM. TKTS accepts only cash or traveler's checks—no checks or credit cards.

The Duffy Square lines are long but congenial, with street entertainers galore and envoys from some of the shows trying to lure you out of line with no-wait discounts. It may be worth a trip to the World Trade Center or Brooklyn TKTS so you can save the waiting time and plan the remainder of the afternoon around your evening at the theater.

Concerts

Much of New York's serious music scene clusters around the magnificent concert halls and theaters of Lincoln Center (Broadway and 65th St., tel. 212/877–2011). **Avery Fisher Hall** (tel. 212/874–2424) is the home of the New York Philharmonic Orchestra, the American Philharmonic, the Mostly Mozart festival, and visiting orchestras and soloists. Smaller **Alice Tully Hall** (tel. 212/362–1911), in the Juilliard School of Music building, features chamber music and jazz performances. Although most tickets are sold on a subscription basis, individual seats may be available at the box office in advance or through Centercharge (tel. 212/874–6770).

Since 1891, playing **Carnegie Hall** (Seventh Ave. and 57th St., tel. 212/247–7800) has epitomized a musician's ascent to the big time. Now it presents visiting orchestras, recitals, chamber music, and pop concerts. The **Weill Recital Hall** features lesser-known artists at lower prices. Student/senior rush tickets are available from 6 PM on performance nights. Public tours are given on Tuesday and Thursday; call 212/247–7800 for information.

Merkin Concert Hall (129 W. 67th St., tel. 212/362–8719) is a reasonably priced stop on the concert circuit. Though threatened with gentrification-motivated demolition, **Symphony Space** (2537 Broadway at 95th St., tel. 212/864–5400) continues to present an eclectic program of concerts, literary readings, dance, and drama at painless (free–$20) prices. The **Metropolitan Museum of Art** (Fifth Ave. and 82nd St., tel. 212/570–3949) hosts a concert series in its 708-seat auditorium. The **92nd Street Y** (YM-YWHA, 1395 Lexington Ave. at 92nd St., tel. 212/996–1100) offers chamber music and recitals by top-name musicians.

Concerts are also performed regularly at churches, colleges, museums, recital halls, lofts, and other spaces throughout the city. To find out when and where, consult the Music and Dance section of *New York* magazine, the Sunday *New York Times* Arts & Leisure section, or listings in the *New Yorker*.

A TKTS-like operation called **Bryant Park Half-Price Tickets** sells discount day-of-performance tickets for music and dance concerts all over the city—including Lincoln Center and Carnegie

Hall. Tickets cost half the regular price plus a $1.50 service charge. *42nd St. just east of Sixth Ave., tel. 212/382-2323. Open Tues., Thurs., Fri., noon-2, 3-7; Wed. & Sat. 11-2, 3-7; Sun. noon-6. Cash or traveler's checks only.*

Opera

The **Metropolitan Opera House** (Broadway and 65th St., tel. 212/362-6000), at Lincoln Center, is a sublime setting for mostly classic operas performed by world-class stars. Tickets can be expensive—up to $90—and hard to get, but low-price standing-room tickets may be available.

New York City Opera (Broadway and 65th St., tel. 212/870-5570), at the State Theater, Lincoln Center, is a first-class opera company with lower ticket prices—under $50—and an innovative and unpredictable schedule.

Other New York opera companies include the **Amato Opera Theater** (319 Bowery near 2nd St., tel. 212/228-8200), a downtown showcase for young performers. The **Light Opera Company of Manhattan** (Playhouse 91, 316 E. 91st. St., tel. 212/831-2000) presents energetic versions of Gilbert and Sullivan operettas throughout the year. Other companies produce operas on an irregular basis throughout the year: Check *New York* magazine or the *New York Times* for current productions.

Dance

The **American Ballet Theatre** (Broadway and 65th St., tel. 212/362-6000) under the direction of Mikhail Baryshnikov is the resident company of the Metropolitan Opera House in Lincoln Center. ABT mingles classics with new ballets during the spring (May–June) season. Ticket prices start low, around $8 for standing room, and rise to over $50.

The renowned **New York City Ballet** (Broadway and 65th St., tel. 212/870-5570), a resident of Lincoln Center's New York State Theater, reached world-class prominence under the direction of George Balanchine. The largest dance organization in the Western World (107 dancers) performs a spring season in May and June, and a winter program from November through February. Tickets range from $6 to $45.

A Moorish-style former Masonic temple, the **City Center Theater** (131 W. 55th St., tel. 212/581–7907) hosts innovative modern dance companies like the Alvin Ailey troupe, the Paul Taylor Company, and the experimentally minded Joffrey Ballet. The **Joyce Theater** (175 Eighth Ave. at 19th St., tel. 212/242–0800) is an Art Deco former movie house with a contemporary fall and spring season; it is also the New York home of the Eliot Feld dance company. Nearby, the **Dance Theater Workshop** (219 W. 19th St., tel. 212/924–0077) is a second-floor performance space that highlights the work of avant-garde dancers and choreographers. The 127-year-old **Brooklyn Academy of Music** (BAM; 30 Lafayette Ave., tel. 718/636–4100) presents programs of ballet and modern dance, and a futuristic Next Wave Festival each fall.

Weekly listings of ballet, modern, and folk dance performances can be found in *New York* magazine and the Arts and Leisure section of the Sunday *New York Times*. Half-price day-of-performance tickets are available at **Bryant Park Half-Price Tickets** (*see* Concerts section for details).

Film

Few cities rival New York's selection of films. Along with all the first-run Hollywood features, an incomparable selection of foreign films, classics, documentaries, and experimental works are playing all over town. The daily *New York Daily News* and *New York Newsday*, the Friday *New York Times*, and the weekly (available Wednesday) *Village Voice* publish schedules and show times for Manhattan movies. *New York* magazine and the *New Yorker* publish programs and capsule reviews but no schedules.

The vast majority of Manhattan theaters are first-run houses. Most charge $7 a ticket for adults at all times; some offer off-peak discounts for children and seniors. Even though New York has recently lost some of its venerable revival houses (the Thalia, the Regency), many remaining theaters still feature revivals, classics, and off-beat films.

The **Film Forum 1 & 2** (209 W. Hudson St., tel. 212/431–1590) in SoHo features contemporary foreign films, documentaries, and other unusual work. The **Thalia Soho** (15 Vandam St. near Sixth Ave., tel. 212/675–0498) has six weekly double-feature revivals and retrospectives. The **Bleecker Street Cinemas** (144 Bleecker St., tel. 212/674–2560) in Greenwich Village have foreign and American favorites, often double features. **Cinema Village** (22 E. 12th St., tel. 212/924–3363) changes its programs of double-feature revivals four times a week. **Theatre 80** (80 St. Marks Pl., tel. 212/254–7400) in the East Village has different double-feature revival programs nearly every day. The **Public Theater** (425 Lafayette St., tel. 212/598–7171) concentrates on retrospectives and documentaries.

The **Museum of Modern Art** (11 W. 53rd St., tel. 212/708–9490) shows film classics every day in two theaters; movies are free with museum admission. The **Whitney Museum** (945 Madison Ave. at 75th St., tel. 212/570–0537) showcases independent American films; admission is free with museum admission. The **Collective for Living Cinema** (41 White St., tel. 212/925–2111) in TriBeCa has an ambitious, constantly changing program of experimental films.

Some foreign cultural institutions show films in their respective languages, with subtitles. They include the **French Institute** (22 E. 60th St., tel. 212/355–6100); the German **Goethe House** (1014 Fifth Ave. at 82nd St., tel. 212/972–3960); and **Japan House** (333 E. 47th St., tel. 212/832–1155).

Nightlife

Cabaret

The Ballroom. A Chelsea tapas (Spanish appetizers) bar with top-name cabaret acts and outrageous revues. *253 W. 28th St., tel. 212/244–3005. Sets at 6:30, 9, 11. AE, MC, V.*

Broadway Baby. A piano bar featuring performing waiters and waitresses. *407 Amsterdam Ave. at 79th St., tel. 212/724-6868. Open 8 PM-4 AM. AE.*

Catch A Rising Star. Continuous comedy by performers on their way up—or down. *1487 First Ave. near 78th St., tel. 212/794-1906. Shows Sun.-Thurs. at 9, Fri., Sat. at 7:30, 10, and 12:30. AE.*

Don't Tell Mama. Lively piano bar up front with no cover or minimum and chancey "open mike" policy. Cabaret performers work the back room. *343 W. 46th St., tel. 212/757-0788. Shows 8 and 10. No credit cards.*

The Duplex. A bilevel Village club with torch singers and hot comics. *55 Grove St., tel. 212/255-5438. Shows at 8, 10, and midnight Fri. and Sat. No credit cards.*

Eleonora. An Italian restaurant with a variety of entertainers nightly except Sunday. *117 W. 58th St., tel. 212/765-1427. Open nightly until midnight. AE, CB, DC, MC, V.*

Greene Street. Posh two-level SoHo restaurant where a second-floor cabaret features singers or comics on Friday and Saturday nights. *105 Greene St., tel. 212/925-2415. Cabaret open Fri. and Sat. 8 PM-1:30 AM. AE, CB, DC, MC, V.*

Jan Wallman's. Hot restaurant-cabaret on the ground floor of the Hotel Iroquois features jazz-oriented singers and players. *49 W. 44th St., tel. 212/764-8930. Shows Mon.-Sat. at 9 and 11. AE, CB, DC, MC, V.*

The Original Improvisation. New York's original comedy showcase where all the big-name yucksters (Rodney Dangerfield, Richard Pryor, Robert Klein) earned their first giggles. *358 W. 44th St., tel. 212/765-8268. Shows Sun.-Thurs. at 9; Fri. 9 and 11:30; Sat. 8, 10, and 12:40. AE.*

Steve McGraw's (formerly Palsson's). West Side showroom presents scathingly irreverent satirical revues and cabaret shows. *158 W. 72nd St., tel. 212/595-7400. Two shows nightly; call for times and reservations. AE, CB, DC, MC, V.*

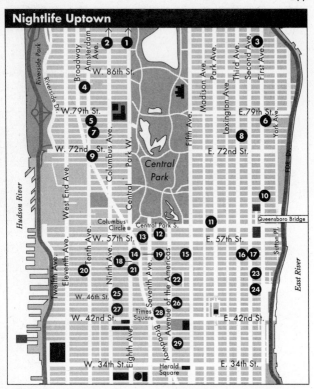

Nightlife Uptown

Abbey, **1**

Broadway
Baby, **5**

Catch a Rising
Star, **6**

Don't Tell
Mama, **25**

Eleonora, **12**

Hard Rock
Cafe, **13**

Hideaway, **29**

The Original
Improvisation, **27**

Jan
Wallman's, **26**

J.G. Melon, **7, 8**

Lone Star
Roadhouse, **18**

Michael's
Pub, **17**

Mikell's, **2**

P.J. Clarke's, **16**

Raccoon
Lodge, **4, 59**

Rainbow
Room, **22**

The Red
Zone, **19**

Regines, **11**

The Ritz, **14**

Roseland, **21**

Runyon's, **23, 24**

Shout!, **28**

Soundscape, **20**

Steve
McGraw's, **9**

The Surf Club, **3**

T.G.I.
Friday's, **10**

Top of the
Sixes, **15**

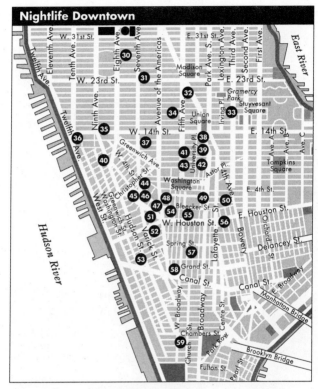

Nightlife Downtown

Angry
Squire, **31**

The Ballroom, **30**

The Bitter
End, **55**

Blue Note, **48**

Bolido, **34**

Bottom Line, **47**

Bradley's, **41**

Caramba!, **49**

Cat Club, **38**

CBGB, **50**

Cedar
Tavern, **39**

The Duplex, **45**

Eagle Tavern, **35**

Ear Inn, **53**

Fat
Tuesday's, **33**

Greene
Street, **57**

Island Club, **58**

Knickerbocker
Bar & Grill, **43**

Knitting
Factory, **56**

Lion's Head, **44**

Mars, **36**

McSorley's Old
Ale House, **42**

S.O.B.'s, **52**

Stringfellow's, **32**

Sweet Basil, **51**

Village Gate, **54**

Village
Vanguard, **46**

White Horse
Tavern, **40**

Zinno's, **37**

Jazz Clubs

Most jazz clubs have substantial cover charges and a drink minimum for table service. You can usually save one or both of these charges by sitting at or standing around the bar.

In Greenwich Village, the **Village Vanguard** (178 Seventh Ave. S, tel. 212/255–4037) is a basement joint that has ridden the crest of every new wave in jazz for over 50 years. The **Village Gate** (160 Bleecker St., tel. 212/475–5120) can present different jazz-related acts and shows simultaneously in three places. No cover on the Village Gate terrace. Go to **Sweet Basil** (88 Seventh Ave. S near Bleecker St., tel. 212/242–1785) for a roomful of jazz memorabilia and top-name groups. **Zinno's** (126 W. 13th St., tel. 212/924–5182) serves moderately priced Italian meals along with mainstream jazz.

The **Blue Note** (131 W. 3rd St., tel. 212/475–8592) is a new incarnation of a legendary jazz club. Smoky and crowded, **Bradley's** (70 University Pl., tel. 212/228–6440) is a low-key place that spotlights piano-and-bass combos. The **Knitting Factory** (47 E. Houston St., tel. 212/219–3055), a hot new place on the frontier of SoHo, features avant-garde groups. The **Knickerbocker Bar & Grill** (33 University Pl., tel. 212/228–8490) presents cool jazz in a noisy Olde New York setting.

Farther uptown, **Angry Squire** (216 Seventh Ave. near 23rd St., tel. 212/242–9066) is a Chelsea neighborhood pub with contemporary sounds from small groups. Cozy **Fat Tuesday's** (190 Third Ave. at 17th St., tel. 212/533–7902) is an intimate downstairs place where jazz superstars play. Latin rhythms fill the air at **Soundscape** (500 W. 52nd St., tel. 212/242–3374). **Michael's Pub** (211 E. 55th St., tel. 212/758–2272) has mainstream jazz, top vocalists, jazz-based revues—and Woody Allen's Dixieland band most Mondays.

On the Upper West Side, go to **Mikell's** (760 Columbus Ave. at 97th St., tel. 212/864–8832) for a variety of jazz-influenced sounds.

Pop and Rock Clubs

The *Village Voice* carries the best listings of who's playing where on the pop and rock scene.

In Greenwich Village, **The Bottom Line** (15 W. 4th St. off Mercer St., tel. 212/228–6300) offers rock, jazz, country/western music, or comedy nightly. For over 25 years **The Bitter End** (147 Bleecker St., tel. 212/673–7030) has been giving a break to folk, rock, jazz, comedy, and country acts. Everyone goes to the **Cat Club** (76 E. 13th St., tel. 212/505–0090) for dancing, swing music, and rock 'n' roll. A low-key Irish pub, the **Eagle Tavern** (355 W. 14th St., tel. 212/924–0275) presents traditional Irish music Monday and Friday, and comedy on Tuesday, Thursday, and Sunday.

South of the Village, the **Island Club** (285 West Broadway at Canal St., tel. 212/226–4598) spotlights reggae, calypso, salsa, and soul. **S.O.B.'s** (Sounds of Brazil; 204 Varick St., tel. 212/243–4940) is a sophisticated tropical setting for south-of-the-border music. **CBGB** (315 Bowery, tel. 212/982–4052) still blasts eardrums with the hard rock sound of heavy metal.

Farther uptown, **The Ritz** (254 W. 54th St., tel. 212/541–8900) is a restored Art Deco ballroom that hosts the newest rock groups. **The Lone Star Roadhouse** (240 W. 52nd St., tel. 212/245–2950) offers big names in country swing and big city blues.

Discos and Dance Clubs

A swank showcase for the Italian design style known as Bolidismo, its creator describes **Bolido** (3 W. 18th St., tel. 212/463–8898) as a "George Jetson fantasy." Occupying an old meat-packing warehouse, **Mars** (10th Ave. at 13th St., tel. 212/691–6262) was redone à la early urban decay; take your pick among five levels. The door staff is *very* particular. Opened in January 1989, **The Red Zone** (440 W. 54th St., tel. 212/582–2222), a 14,000-square-foot discotheque, features huge movie screens where images of water-lapped beaches and the Wild West are projected. At **The Surf Club** (416 E.

91st St., tel. 212/410–1360), the East Side upper crust lets down its hair (though managing even in the heat of the moment to remain impeccably coiffed).

For "touch dancing" the way they used to do it, 70-year-old **Roseland** (239 W. 52nd St., tel. 212/247–0200) has two orchestras Thursday through Sunday nights and matinees from 2:30 PM. The **Hideaway** (32 W. 37th St., tel. 212/947–8940), in what was once John Barrymore's town house, features singers and small groups for close-up dancing. At elegant **Regines** (502 Park Ave. at 59th St., tel. 212/826–0990) an expensive dinner buys access to the disco floor—or you can eat elsewhere and pay a cover charge. Most spectacular of all, the newly remodeled **Rainbow Room** atop the 65-floor RCA Building (30 Rockefeller Center, tel. 212/632–5100) gives you a dance floor straight out of the Hollywood classics.

Clubs and Bars for Singles (Under 30)

Downtown, the postcollege generation gathers at the pointedly casual **Raccoon Lodge** (59 Warren St., tel. 212/766–9656), named after the fraternal affiliation of Ralph Kramden and Ed Norton. A newer branch of the Lodge recently opened on the Upper West Side (480 Amsterdam Ave. at 83rd St., tel. 212/874–9984). The **Ear Inn** (326 Spring St. near Greenwich St., tel. 212/226–9060) boasts an archetypal juke box and regular poetry readings. Young people throng to **McSorley's Old Ale House** (15 E. 7th St., tel. 212/473–9148), one of the oldest and most crowded bars in the city. **Caramba!** (684 Broadway at Third St., tel. 212/420–9817) serves tropical concoctions and Mexican food to a cocktail-hour crowd that never wants to go home.

Farther uptown, lines are usually waiting outside the **Hard Rock Cafe** (221 W. 57th St., tel. 212/489–6565), a shrine to rock 'n' roll. The nine-to-five crowd unwinds to '50s and '60s tunes at **Shout!** (124 W. 43rd St., tel. 212/869–2088). On the Upper East Side, **T.G.I.Friday's** (1152 First Ave. at 63rd St., tel. 212/832–8512) has a long tradition as a congenial gathering place. On the

Upper West Side, young crowds congregate at the **Abbey** (237 W. 105th St., tel. 212/222–8713).

Clubs and Bars for Singles (Over 30)

Three traditional Greenwich Village literary hangouts continue to attract local regulars and curious visitors. The **Lion's Head** (59 Christopher St. off Seventh Ave. S, (tel. 212/929–0670) is a well-worn basement spot still popular with local scribes. The **White Horse Tavern** (567 Hudson St. and 11th St., tel. 212/243–9260), which figures prominently in the legend and lore of Dylan Thomas, now has outdoor seating during summer. The **Cedar Tavern** (82 University Pl., tel. 212/929–9089) was a haunt of beatnik writers and abstract expressionist painters.

Farther uptown, **Stringfellows** (35 E. 21st St., tel. 212/254–2444), an upscale bar, restaurant, and dance club, stays hopping with British and American sounds until the wee, wee hours. The two **Runyon's** (305 E. 50th St., tel. 212/223–9592; and 932 Second Ave. near 49th St., tel. 212/759–7800) claim the prize as the city's primo sports bars. **P. J. Clarke's** (915 Third Ave. at 55th St., tel. 212/759–1650) has a welcoming old-time decor and serves great bar food. On the 39th floor of 666 Fifth Avenue, **Top of the Sixes** (tel. 212/757–6662) offers 360-degree views to a large cocktail-hour crowd. East Side, West Side, the **J. G. Melon** establishments (1291 Third Ave. at 74th St., tel. 212/650–1310; and 340 Amsterdam Ave. at 76th St., tel. 212/877–2220) are comfortable, low-pressure places where you can meet people.

Personal Itinerary

Departure *Date*

Time

Transportation

HOTEL ROOSEVELT.
MADISON AVE AT 45th St.

Arrival *Date*   *Time*

Departure *Date*   *Time*

Transportation

Arrival *Date*   *Time*

Departure *Date*   *Time*

Transportation

Arrival *Date*   *Time*

Departure *Date*   *Time*

Transportation

Personal Itinerary

Arrival *Date*   *Time*

Departure *Date*   *Time*

Transportation

Arrival *Date*   *Time*

Departure *Date*   *Time*

Transportation

Arrival *Date*   *Time*

Departure *Date*   *Time*

Transportation

Arrival *Date*   *Time*

Departure *Date*   *Time*

Transportation

Personal Itinerary

Arrival *Date*　　　　*Time*

Departure *Date*　　　*Time*

Transportation

Arrival *Date*　　　　*Time*

Departure *Date*　　　*Time*

Transportation

Arrival *Date*　　　　*Time*

Departure *Date*　　　*Time*

Transportation

Arrival *Date*　　　　*Time*

Departure *Date*　　　*Time*

Transportation

Adresses

Name

Address

Telephone

Name

Address

Telephone

Name

Address

Telephone

Name

Address

Telephone

Name

Address

Telephone

Name

Address

Telephone

Adresses

Name

Address

Telephone

Name

Address

Telephone

Name

Address

Telephone

Name

Address

Telephone

Name

Address

Telephone

Name

Address

Telephone

Fodor's Travel Guides

U.S. Guides

Alaska
Arizona
Atlantic City & the
  New Jersey Shore
Boston
California
Cape Cod
Carolinas & the
  Georgia Coast
The Chesapeake Region
Chicago
Colorado
Dallas & Fort
  Worth

Disney World & the
  Orlando Area
Florida
Hawaii
Houston &
  Galveston
Las Vegas
Los Angeles, Orange
  County, Palm Springs
Maui
Miami, Fort Lauderdale,
  Palm Beach
Michigan, Wisconsin,
  Minnesota

New England
New Mexico
New Orleans
New Orleans (Pocket
  Guide)
New York City
New York City (Pocket
  Guide)
New York State
Pacific North Coast
Philadelphia
The Rockies
San Diego
San Francisco

San Francisco (Pocket
  Guide)
The South
Texas
USA
Virgin Islands
Virginia
Waikiki
Washington, DC
Williamsburg

Foreign Guides

Acapulco
Amsterdam
Australia, New Zealand,
  The South Pacific
Austria
Bahamas
Bahamas (Pocket
  Guide)
Baja & the Pacific
  Coast Resorts
Barbados
Beijing, Guangzhou &
  Shanghai
Belgium &
  Luxembourg
Bermuda
Brazil
Britain (Great Travel
  Values)
Budget Europe
Canada
Canada (Great Travel
  Values)
Canada's Atlantic
  Provinces
Cancun, Cozumel,
  Yucatan Peninsula

Caribbean
Caribbean (Great
  Travel Values)
Central America
Eastern Europe
Egypt
Europe
Europe's Great
  Cities
Florence & Venice
France
France (Great Travel
  Values)
Germany
Germany (Great Travel
  Values)
Great Britain
Greece
The Himalayan
  Countries
Holland
Hong Kong
Hungary
India, including Nepal
Ireland
Israel
Italy

Italy (Great Travel
  Values)
Jamaica
Japan
Japan (Great Travel
  Values)
Jordan & the
  Holy Land
Kenya, Tanzania,
  the Seychelles
Korea
Lisbon
Loire Valley
London
London (Great
  Travel Values)
London (Pocket Guide)
Madrid & Barcelona
Mexico
Mexico City
Montreal &
  Quebec City
Munich
New Zealand
North Africa
Paris
Paris (Pocket Guide)

People's Republic of
  China
Portugal
Rio de Janeiro
The Riviera (Fun on)
Rome
Saint Martin &
  Sint Maarten
Scandinavia
Scandinavian Cities
Scotland
Singapore
South America
South Pacific
Southeast Asia
Soviet Union
Spain
Spain (Great Travel
  Values)
Sweden
Switzerland
Sydney
Tokyo
Toronto
Turkey
Vienna
Yugoslavia

Special-Interest Guides

Health & Fitness
  Vacations
Royalty Watching

Selected Hotels of
  Europe

Selected Resorts and
  Hotels of the U.S.
Shopping in Europe

Skiing in North America
Sunday in New York